LIVING ENGLISH SPEECH

SPEECH

STRESS AND INTONATION PRACTICE FOR THE FOREIGN STUDENT

By

W. STANNARD ALLEN, B.A. (LOND.)

LONGMANS

LONGMANS, GREEN & CO. LTD.,

London and Harlow

Associated companies, branches and representatives throughout the world.

First published 1954
New edition *1965
New impression *October* 1966
New impression *April* 1967
New impression 1969

SBN 582 52361 3

PRINTED IN HONG KONG
BY DAI NIPPON PRINTING CO. (INTERNATIONAL) LTD.

CONTENTS
(Subject-matter of the exercises)

EXERCISES RECORDED ON TAPE

Tape 1

8	14	15	37	42	43	44	46	47
48	50	54	55	59	60	61	62	64
67	68	70	81	82	84	85	86	

Tape 2

87	91	94	99	100	107	109
111	114	119	124	129	130	132
136	137	138	139	141	142	145

and MUM'S THE WORD.

These two tapes are recorded (top-track only) at $3\frac{3}{4}$ i.p.s. (9·5 cm. p.s.) on five-inch (13 cm.) reels of LP polyester tape and may be ordered from booksellers.

We are indebted to the Proprietors of *Punch* for permission to include *Mum's the Word*, by Marjorie Riddell, which appeared in the issue of March 4th, 1953.

WHAT THIS BOOK IS ABOUT

This book is designed for use in English classes for foreign students, its purpose being to present the basic principles of stress and intonation and to provide copious practical exercises. The vocabulary of the exercises is deliberately simple, many of them being quite suitable for students who have been learning for less than six months.

This book is not a course in itself, but rather a graded set of supplementary exercises for providing practice in stress, rhythm and intonation at all stages of learning English. The notes and remarks are intended for the teacher, to acquaint him with the point of each exercise and suggest how it might be practised. Exercises appropriate to the standard of the class can be worked through as part of the conversation or spoken English hour, preceded where necessary by a blackboard exposition of the points to be practised.

Apart from the stress exercises with polysyllabic words, the vocabulary of even the advanced exercises is fairly simple. As this book is intended for the use of all types of foreign students of English, and not only students specializing in the language, it has not been written in a phonetic script. Examples and exercises are in the normal orthography apart from a few isolated instances, where a broad type of transcription (as found in Daniel Jones's Pronouncing Dictionary) is used. It would be an unnecessary obstacle to the average student if he had to learn to read a phonetic script fluently first. The diacritics necessary as a guide to the required stress or intonation have been added to a normal script, and by combining these with certain typographical devices it has been possible to present even complex patterns in the form of exercises that are readily understood.

I must conclude these introductory remarks with sincere thanks to the many anonymous students who have unwittingly contributed to the book whenever they opened their mouths; to my wife for providing a lot of extra practice material; and to Milica Rekalić of Belgrade for devoting so many of her spare hours to making a typed draft from my original hieroglyphics, a feat only possible to one brought up on cursive cyrillics.

W. S. ALLEN

Belgrade
April 1953

RECORDINGS ON TAPE

Two tapes are now available for use with this book in the language laboratory or with a tape recorder in the classroom (or for private study and practice). A representative selection of exercises (see p. iv for a complete list) are presented in a practical way, first providing a model pattern and then practising the pattern by means of pauses for repetition by the student. In this new edition of the book the examples chosen for recording are printed first in each exercise. Between six and ten examples are recorded in these exercises (and the remainder may be completed by the teacher with the class).

BOOK LIST

Although a number of familiar intonation patterns in English appears for the first time in this book as deliberate practice material, the general background of this subject has already been covered in many books and articles. On these the writer of this book has based many of the exercises, and students or teachers who are curious to make a more detailed examination of this aspect of English should consult the standard textbooks on the subject. The following books would probably be the most useful for an average general student:

D. JONES: *Outline of English Phonetics*, Ch. 28–31 (Heffer).

ARMSTRONG AND WARD: *Handbook of English Intonation* (Heffer).

IDA WARD: *Phonetics of English*, Ch. 15–16 (Heffer).

PALMER AND BLANDFORD: *Everyday Sentences in Spoken English* (Heffer).

R. LAS VERGNAS: *Les pièges de l'anglais parlé* (Hachette).

KENNETH L. PIKE: *The Intonation of American English* (Univ. of Michigan).

ROGER KINGDON: *The Groundwork of English Intonation* and *English Intonation Practice* (Longmans).

SUMMARY OF NOTATION AND TYPOGRAPHY

The following list of signs and types is for reference only. More detailed explanation is given in the notes to the appropriate exercises.

Stress and rhythm

ˈ is placed before a syllable or word having stress. E.g. beˈfore.

□□□□ pictorial representation of rhythmic groups of **stressed** syllables (big squares) and **unstressed** syllables (little squares).

E.g. ˈtake it aˈway □□□□

Music notation is used in addition where it is necessary to show the exact stress-pattern or uneven rhythms.

E.g. $\frac{2}{4}$ ♫ | ♩ ⁊ | in a ˈbook

$\frac{2}{4}$ | ♫ ♩ | ˈattitude

$\frac{2}{4}$ | ♪. ♪ ♩ | ˈaptitude

Intonation

Introductory unstressed syllables are printed in *italics*.

The stressed syllable that begins a fall or a rise in the tune is printed in **bold type**.

The accent to indicate this fall is ˋ

The accent to indicate this rise is ˏ

A new high pitch in longer sentences is preceded by ↑

Examples: *He will* ˈcome toˋday.
ˈCan you ˈcome toˏday?
He ˈasked us to ˈtell him the ↑ ˈright way to ˋdo it.

The intonation of the model sentence at the beginning of each exercise is also shown graphically between two parallel lines. These lines represent the approximate upper and lower limits of the voice, with dashes to show stressed syllables, and dots to show unstressed ones. The three examples just used would be shown graphically as follows:

(a) *He will* ˈcome toˋday.

(b) ˈCan you ˈcome toˏday?

(c) *He* ˈasked us to ˈtell him the ↑ ˈright way to ˋdo it.

Syllables taking a stress in order to convey a special meaning, that is, in order to give them particular prominence in the speaker's thoughts, are printed in CAPITALS.

Example: *But he wrote* ˋYOUR name in ˋMY book.

The above sentence shown graphically:

But he wrote ˋYOUR name in ˋMY book.

This kind of stress, when occurring together with a

rising intonation, produces the characteristic wave (fall-rise) that is found at the end of so many English sentences. It is printed here as follows:—

Example: *But I* `CAN'T come to`DAY.

The above sentence shown graphically:

> *But I* `CAN'T come to`DAY.

The division between two intonation patterns in one sentence is shown by a vertical stroke.

Example: *They were* |too `late | ,weren't they?

The above sentence shown graphically:

> *They were* |too `late, ,weren't they?

INTRODUCTORY NOTES

An English course for foreigners must necessarily concentrate on the structure of the English language. It cannot teach much about the spoken language apart from offering a guide to pronunciation. Most of the practical work in spoken English must be devised by the teacher; normally he uses either more or less spoken English in his classes in proportion to his own ability in the language. This book is designed to give systematic practice in the spoken language. It assumes a basic knowledge of the sounds of English and provides graded exercises in the less easily defined world of stress, rhythm and intonation.

Stress, rhythm and intonation should really be considered as a whole, for they are very closely connected elements of a single aspect of the language that we might call Speech Flow. Speech is essentially movement. However accurately we learn to pronounce the isolated sounds of a language we must still train ourselves to set them in motion in the right manner if we wish to make ourselves easily understood. A student of music learns the theory of combining sounds into harmonic sequences, yet he does not create music until he can make this material move in a melodic shape. Music has its Stress in the regular recurrence of beats; it has its own Rhythm; and melody is its Intonation. Spoken language behaves in a broadly similar way. The sounds of English and isolated syllables, like notes or chords in music, only become intelligible when set in motion. This movement—its beats, its rhythms and its melody—

is the theme that this book develops throughout its series of controlled exercises.

Broadly speaking, a reasonably correct speech-flow is more important for intelligibility than correct sounds. It is possible to carry on an intelligible English conversation in a series of mumbles and grunts, provided the voice-movement is correct. English people often do this when exchanging a few words on a trivial topic, though we do not suggest that foreign students should take examples of this kind of intercourse as their models. On the other hand, some foreign speakers of English, even though they learn to make English sounds quite well, fail to acquire a sufficiently accurate speech-flow. The result is that English-speaking people find it quite difficult to understand them; and they, for their part, complain that English people mispronounce or swallow half their words.

This book consists of exercises on all the aspects of spoken English that contain problems for a foreign student. There are, however, no drills on individual sounds. Most class text-books on modern lines contain sufficient practice material on the sounds themselves.[1] Here you will find material to practise typical English speech patterns. Although it is wiser not to make a rigid division between the elements of Stress, Rhythm and Intonation, this book does in fact present its exercises to the student in that order. The earlier exercises are purely on the stressing of words in phrases and sentences; this leads to speech rhythms, with exercises on typical English rhythmic patterns; and the final (and longest) section of the book deals with intonation, presupposing some knowledge of stress and rhythm.

Nevertheless, teachers will find that exercises can be

---

[1] The graded pronunciation drills that run through the first three books of the well-known *Essential English* method, by C. E. Eckersley (Longmans, Green), provide an excellent example of this.

practised from all three sections simultaneously. The vocabulary is simple and up-to-date; and, except for the exercises on the secondary stress of long words, it is well within the range of fairly elementary students.

The book is not intended to be "worked through" in the manner of an ordinary text-book. An exercise or two should be used at every opportunity for oral practice as part of the classwork in spoken English. An important feature of a large number of the exercises, especially those on stress and rhythm, is repetition. Phrases or patterns are to be repeated two or three times, and the teacher must insist on unhurried regularity, taking care to start off the next phrase himself at the same regular pace. This kind of exercise can be kept steady more easily by practising a group of people rather than individual students. The tapping of a ruler or pencil, or hand movement as for the restrained conducting of a choir, will certainly be needed from time to time.

If any real progress is to be made towards a type of spoken English that sounds natural, faulty speech-flow should be corrected at every opportunity; an exercise in grammar done orally should at the same time be treated as an exercise in the spoken language. It is important to start good habits right from the very first lessons, for five minutes' drill in the early stages is worth fifty minutes at a later stage when bad habits have already been allowed to form.[1] It is not necessary to spend too much time on trying to perfect the pronunciation of elementary students, but they *should* be made to imitate the broader features of the spoken language whenever they use it. By spending too much time on the sounds of English in the early stages of

[1] *Oxford Progressive English for Adult Learners*, by A. S. Hornby, published by Oxford University Press, 1953, has work on stress and in- tonation as an integral part of the early stages of learning.

learning the language a student will fail to see the wood for the trees; for the key to intelligibility lies more in knowing how to move the voice according to accepted patterns of stress and melody than in making or recognizing correctly the component sounds.

STRESS AND RHYTHM

When English is spoken, we can hear that some syllables stand out above the others. This can be quite an objective feature of speech, since it is just as marked when reading a list of words from a dictionary as when we are engaged in conversation. We can also give special point to our ideas by stressing certain vital words as we speak. In print we put words specially stressed in this way in italics, or in writing a personal letter we can underline such words when we wish to be sure that the reader has exactly the shade of meaning we wish to express. This special stress for emphasis, unlike the natural stress of words in an objective setting, usually affects the intonation. For this reason exercises on it are delayed until the appropriate place among exercises on intonation.

We shall begin with exercises on the stress and rhythm of words in phrases and sentences. (The complicated subject of the correct stressing of individual words of several syllables will be found as an appendix with further exercises at the back of the book.) Spoken English shows a marked contrast between its stressed (strong) and unstressed (weak) syllables, a fact which largely accounts for its characteristic rhythmic patterns. Some languages[1] make very little difference between syllables in the matter of stress. Native speakers of such languages find it especially difficult to achieve a natural speech-flow in English; they would be advised, therefore, to do the stress and rhythm exercises carefully and to return to them from time to time.

[1] e.g. French.

I

For the sake of the exercises that comprise the greater part of this book, work on stress and rhythm has been somewhat artificially separated from that on intonation. It is stress, however, that largely dictates the significant moves of the voice up or down, and an ability to stress a phrase correctly will help to guide the speaker to use the correct intonation, for the voice changes its direction only on stressed syllables. Stress and rhythm are even more closely connected; we might draw a useful musical parallel by likening stress to the main beats or pulse, and rhythm to the various patterns of movement that fill the spaces from one pulse to another. One cannot rely too much on this musical analogy, however, since the pulse and rhythm of conversational speech or of prose-reading will be of a much freer pattern than the more regularly recurring musical bars. Nevertheless, for the sake of practice, many of the exercises that follow should be done under a kind of musical discipline with an insistence on rhythmic regularity.

Sentence stress

It can be generally assumed that in any normal sentence we shall stress (or give full sound value to) the *significant* words only. These are briefly:

1. Nouns (and some pronouns, notably interrogatives).
2. Demonstratives (this, that, etc.).
3. Adjectives.
4. Most adverbs.
5. Verbs (and auxiliaries in certain circumstances).

The other words in a sentence, mostly form-words to join together the words that carry meaning, are normally unstressed, many of them having special weak forms. Prepositions, auxiliaries, conjunctions and pronouns make up the greater part. The syllables bearing stress proceed at a fairly regular pace, the unstressed syllables being accommodated between them in varying rhythmic sequences. The latter provide one of the greatest difficulties for the foreign student, who generally tries to give them a fuller pronunciation than is due to them.

We can see this most clearly by comparing sentences with many significant words (and therefore many stresses) with sentences consisting mainly of form-words (and therefore of few stresses). Consider the following four sentences: the first and second have 11 and 12 words respectively, 10 of them being stressed; the third and fourth have 14 and 16 words respectively with only 4 stresses each. Yet the *longer* sentences take only half the time to say that the shorter ones take. The unstressed words, crowded together between the steadily moving pulses, are spoken quite quickly compared with the shorter sentences full of the stressed syllables.

1. ˈBert's ˈfriend ˈJohn has ˈjust ˈsold ˈtwo ˈvery ˈfine ˈold ˋpaintings.

2. *The* ˈDaniel ˈJones Proˈnouncing ˈDictionary ˈlists ˈmost ˈversions of ˈmodern ˈEnglish pronunciˋation.

3. ˈWhat would you have ˈdone if he had ˈtalked to you in the ˋstreet?

4. *It would have been* ˈbetter not to have ˈpaid for it beˈfore you had reˋceived it.

The last two in a phonetic transcription:

3. ˈwɔt wud ju əv ˈdʌn if hi əd ˈtɔ:kt tə ju in ðə ˈstri:t.

4. it wud əv bin ˈbetə nɔt tu əv ˈpeid fr it biˈfɔ:jud riˋsi:vd it.

The ability to move smoothly and steadily from one stress to the next, and to fit in the unstressed syllables between them, forms the basis of a good natural English accent. For that reason our first forty exercises or so are devoted to practising points of stress and rhythm only. In all these first exercises the students, whether practising in groups or individually, should aim at regularity and a steady well-accented speed. There should be no attempt to hurry because so many of the exercises seem easy. Group practice is most valuable, possibly more valuable than with single students, and the group should be guided by the teacher. He can do this by "conducting" his choir, or by beating the necessary pulse on his desk. Exercises on stress or rhythm should always be done by repeating each phrase three or four times; care should be taken to keep the rhythm moving smoothly over the whole set of phrases, pausing between each repetition of the phrase if the regularity of the stress seems to require it.

EXERCISES ON STRESS AND RHYTHM

Exercise 1. Adjacent stresses

Note. The following word combinations in English usually have a full stress on each word: adjective-noun; adverb-adjective; adverb-verb. In this exercise the second of the two words is to be read with a falling intonation, viz.:

ǀvery ˋcold

Read each of the following groups three times after the teacher's single reading.

ǀbrown ˋdog, ǀsharp ˋpen, ǀround ˋtable, ǀcurly ˋhair, ǀblue ˋshirt, ǀlarge ˋhouse, ǀbeautiful ˋgirl, ǀgreen ˋgrass, ǀfreshˋ fruit, ǀvery ˋhard, ǀquite ˋpleasant, ǀbadly ˋwritten, ǀnearly ˋfinished, ǀall ˋgone, ǀalmòst ˋeverything, ǀfairly ˋquick, ǀhalf-ˋdressed, ǀwell ˋdone, exǀtremely inˋtelligent, ǀvery exˋpensive, ǀbright ˋlight, ǀsweet ˋvoice, ǀclear ˋsky, ǀbest ˋhat, ǀwrong ˋanswer, ǀgood ˋluck, ǀEnglish ˋlanguage, ǀfar ˋprettier, ǀcarefully preˋpared, ǀbitterly ˋcold, ǀbadly ˋwritten, ǀhot ˋwater, ǀmain ˋroad, ǀheavy ˋtraffic, ǀmodern ˋwriter, ǀquite ˋuseless, ǀheavy ˋrain, ǀBank ˋHoliday, ǀempty ˋbottle, ǀlead ˋpencil.
ǀLeast ǀsaid, ǀsoonest ˋmended.
ǀMore ǀhaste, ǀless ˋspeed.

See also Appendix, Exercise 153, for loss of one stress in certain of the above types because of adjacent stressed words.

Exercise 2. Several adjacent stresses

Note. When several "content" words occur together, care must be taken to give them full stresses. The stressed syllables in this exercise should be spaced in a regular rhythm.

Read the following barred sections. The teacher reads a section once, the students repeat it three times in steady rhythm before the teacher proceeds to the next bar.

1. a ˋbook / a ˈgood ˋbook / a ˈvery ˈgood ˋbook / a ˈvery ˈgood ˋtext-book / a ˈvery ˈgood ˈschool ˋtext-book.

2. a ˋcloth / a ˈpiece of ˋcloth / á ˈpiece of ˈwhite ˋcloth / a ˈlarge ˈpiece of ˈwhite ˋcloth / a ˈlarge ˈpiece of ˈpure ˈwhite ˋcloth.

3. a ˋdoll / ˈMary's ˋdoll / ˈMary's ˈnew ˋdoll / ˈMary's ˈnew ˈchina ˋdoll / ˈMary's ˈtwo ˈnew ˈchina ˋdolls.

4. a ˋboy / a ˈnaughty ˋboy / a ˈvery ˈnaughty ˋboy / a ˈvery ˈnaughty ˈEnglish ˋschoolboy.

5. the ˋday / the ˈwhole ˋday / ˈnearly the ˈwhole ˋday / ˈvery ˈnearly the ˈwhole ˋday / ˈvery ˈnearly the ˈwhole ˈday ˋlong.

6. a ˋcup / an ˈempty ˋcup / an ˈempty ˈcup and ˋsaucer / an ˈempty ˈcup and a ˈbroken ˋsaucer / ˈtwo ˈempty ˈcups and a ˈbroken ˋsaucer.

7. a ˋlorry / a ˈheavy ˋlorry / a ˈheavy ˈlorry with a ˋload / a ˈheavy ˈlorry with a ˈload of ˋwood / a ˈheavy ˈlorry with a ˈfull ˈload of ˋwood / a ˈheavy ˈlorry with a ˈfull ˈload of ˈtwo ˈtons of ˋwood.

8. ˋwhisky / ˈScotch ˋwhisky / a ˈbottle of ˈScotch ˋwhisky / a ˈbottle of ˈgenuine ˈScotch ˋwhisky / ˈhalf a ˈbottle of ˈgenuine ˈScotch ˋwhisky.

9. a ˋclock / my ˈfriend's ˋclock / the ˈhands of my ˈfriend's ˋclock / the ˈmetal ˈhands of my ˈfriend's ˋclock / the ˈtwo ˈbroken ˈmetal ˈhands of my ˈfriend's ˋclock.

10. a ˋhat / a ˈstraw ˋhat / a ˈdirty ˈstraw ˋhat / a ˈvery ˈdirty ˈstraw ˋhat.

11. a ˋchurch / an ˈold ˋchurch / an ˈold ˈCatholic ˋchurch / an ˈold ˈRoman ˈCatholic ˋchurch / a ˈvery ˈold ˈRoman ˈCatholic ˋchurch.

12. ˋshoes / a ˈpair of ˋshoes / a ˈdirty ˈpair of ˋshoes / a ˈdirty ˈpair of ˈbrown ˋshoes / a ˈdirty ˈpair of ˈbrown ˈleather ˋshoes / a ˈvery ˈdirty ˈpair of ˈbrown ˈleather ˋshoes / ˈtwo ˈvery ˈdirty ˈpairs of ˈbrown ˈleather ˋshoes.

13. the ˋpalace / the ˈCrystal ˋPalace / the ˈCrystal ˈPalace Exhiˋbition / the ˈgreat ˈCrystal ˈPalace Exhiˋbition / the ˈgreat ˈCrystal ˈPalace Exhiˋbition of ˈeighteen-fifty-ˋone.

14. a ˋcloth / a ˈlinen ˋcloth / a ˈlinen ˋtable-cloth / a ˈwhite ˈlinen ˋtable-cloth / a ˈclean ˈwhite ˈlinen ˋtable-cloth.

15. ˋsoap-flakes / a ˈsoap-flake ˋpacket / a ˈLux ˈsoap-flake ˋpacket / an ˈempty ˈLux ˈsoap-flake ˋpacket.

16. a ˋdesk / an ˈoak ˋdesk / an ˈoak ˈdesk with ˋdrawers / a ˈpolished ˈoak ˈdesk with ˋdrawers / a ˈpolished ˈoak ˈdesk with ˈlarge ˋdrawers.

17. a ˋtelephone / a ˈpublic ˋtelephone / ˈtwo ˈpublic ˋtelephones / ˈtwo ˈpublic ˈtelephones on ˈPlatform ˋ4 / ˈtwo ˈnew ˈpublic ˈtelephones on ˈPlatform ˋ4.

18. a ˋlight / an eˈlectric ˋlight / an eˈlectric ˈlight with a ˋshade / an eˈlectric ˈlight with a ˈcoloured ˋshade / ˈtwo eˈlectric ˈlights with ˈcoloured ˋshades.

19. a ˋchair / an ˈarmˋchair / ˈGranny's ˈarmˋchair / ˈGranny's ˈfavourite ˈarmˋchair / the ˈback of ˈGranny's ˈfavourite ˈarmˋchair.

20. a ˋpie / an ˈapple ˋpie / a ˈblackberry and ˈapple ˋpie / a ˈlarge ˈblackberry and ˈapple ˋpie / a ˈvery ˈlarge ˈblackberry and ˈapple ˋpie / a ˈvery ˈlarge ˈwell-ˈcooked ˈblackberry and ˈapple ˋpie / a ˈvery ˈlarge ˈwell-ˈcooked ˈblackberry and ˈapple ˈpie with ˈwhipped ˋcream.

Exercise 3. Stress patterns

Note. The next twenty exercises are based on common patterns of stressed and unstressed syllables. They should all be practised in the following manner. In accordance with the key pattern at the head of the exercise, the teacher reads the first phrase and a student (or group of students) repeats it at least three times in succession. The teacher immediately reads the second phrase and the next student (or group) repeats it three times. The whole exercise should be performed in a regular unbroken rhythm as far as possible. In the key patterns a large square indicates a fully stressed syllable and a small square an unstressed or only partially stressed one. To make the method clear, here is the beginning of Exercise 8 as it should sound in a regular rhythm (T=Teacher; S=Students):

Key-pattern: □□□□□   *I've* 'eaten them all.

T. I've eaten them all. S. I've eaten them all, I've eaten

them all, I've eaten them all. T. A beautiful one. S. A

beautiful one, a beautiful one, etc.

Practise in this manner the following series.

Key pattern: □□

come here / look out / what for? / where to? / inside / on top / no more / speak up / sit down / downstairs / say "yes" / try hard / wash up / break down / ask John / go slow / not now / where from? / which one? / hold tight / in time /

no use / please do / no, thanks / yes, please / no good / all
right / run fast / work hard / who's that? / not quite / quite
right / that's true / just then / half way / arm-chair / write
soon / read this.

Exercise 4. Stress patterns

Note. See Exercise 3 for detailed instructions.

Key pattern: ☐□☐

try again / not enough / look inside / show me yours / do
it now / not so fast / lend a hand / cut the bread / make the
tea / run away / go to sleep / have a drink / drive a car /
break it up / what is that? / what's it for? / practise hard /
sing a song / write it down / draw a line / that's a lie / take
it home / have a go / having lunch / who're you? / where's
he from? / hurry up / move along / light the fire / fast
asleep / cold as ice / change your shoes / where's your
hat? / time for bed / here's some tea / lemonade / half an
hour / long ago / can't be done / quite unknown / just in
front / ring me up / ill in bed.

Exercise 5. Stress patterns

Note. See Exercise 3 for detailed instructions.

Key pattern: □☐□

I think so / I thought so / I'd like to / to please them / a
handful / a pity / of course not / I'd love to / he couldn't /
as well as / for ever / they may be / to try it / at breakfast /
the paper / she had to / it's early / she's ready / with
pleasure / I'm sorry / just listen / but why not? / I've
read it / a lot of / without me / in daytime / a nuisance / the
answer / I'd rather / it's broken / in winter.

Exercise 6. Stress patterns

Note. See Exercise 3 for detailed instructions.

Key pattern: ⬜☐⬜☐☐

I ˈthink it is*/ I'd ˈlike you to / to ˈpractise it / a ˈbucketful / it's ˈpossible / we ˈoughtn't to / he ˈwanted it / he
ˈwants us to / they ˈknew it was*/ to ˈborrow it / a ˈlittle
one / a ˈpocketful / a ˈlot of it / they've ˈfinished it / he
ˈthinks he can*/ I ˈthought it was*/ I've ˈheard of it / it
ˈused to be / they ˈmust have been / get ˈrid of it / we
ˈasked them to / he ˈlent me one / he's ˈused to it / let's
ˈgive her some / be ˈnice to her / a ˈfriend of mine / it's
ˈbeautiful / she's ˈpolished them / she ˈcame with us /
beˈcause of it / we ˈspoke to them / I ˈstudied it / there
ˈisn't one / I've ˈpaid for it / chryˈsanthemum / a ˈpair of
them.

* See also Exercise 9 and Exercises 138–40.

Exercise 7. Stress patterns

Note. See Exercise 3 for detailed instructions.

Key pattern: ☐☐☐⬜

ˈwriting it ˈnow / ˈsend him aˈway / ˈreading aˈloud /
ˈterribly ˈslow / ˈgive him a ˈbook / ˈwhat is the ˈtime?/
ˈsing us a ˈsong / ˈrunning aˈway / ˈquick off the ˈmark /
ˈtop of the ˈclass / ˈhardly eˈnough / ˈare you aˈwake?/
ˈthrow it aˈway / ˈsend me a ˈcard / ˈgive me a ˈring /
ˈplaying a ˈgame / ˈmeet me toˈnight / ˈwhere have they
ˈgone?/ ˈwhere have you ˈbeen?/ ˈwhat have you ˈdone?/
ˈwhat is it ˈfor?/ ˈshow me the ˈway / ˈpouring with ˈrain /
ˈgone for a ˈwalk / ˈcome for a ˈswim / ˈheavy as ˈlead /
ˈkilled in the ˈwar / ˈgive him some ˈfood / ˈtime and
aˈgain / ˈnearly as ˈgood / ˈbeautiful ˈgirl / ˈhandsome
young ˈman / ˈno-one is ˈin / ˈcutting the ˈgrass / ˈchop-
ping some ˈwood / ˈleave it aˈlone / ˈnot before ˈtea / ˈready

for ˋlunch / ˈwhen you have ˋtime / ˈnot before ˋthen / ˈwait till I ˋcome / ˈfalling aˋsleep / ˈwhat can you ˋsee? / just for a ˋwhile / ˈwhat did you ˋdo? / ˈget into ˋbed / ˈtop of the ˋhill / ˈleave it beˋhind / ˈdo it aˋgain / ˈwrite it in ˋink / ˈquarter past ˋnine / ˈquarter to ˋten / ˈsee you toˋnight / ˈlots to be ˋdone / ˈnow we're aˋlone / ˈout of the ˋway / ˈcarefully ˋread / ˈswitch off the ˋlight.

Exercise 8. Stress patterns

Note. See Exercise 3 for detailed instructions. In this pattern the voice falls low and stays low after the stress, even if one of the following syllables is partially stressed.

Key pattern: □□□□□

I've ˋeaten them all / a ˋbeautiful one / I ˋpromised him it / to ˋsatisfy them / a ˋtablespoonful / inˋterrogate them / the ˋrailway station / I ˋthink it will be / I ˋthought it had been / he ˋwanted us to / a ˋpenny or two / in ˋspite of it all / he ˋought to have had / a ˋlong time ago / an ˋexercise book / I've ˋwritten to them / we ˋknow what it is / I ˋasked if I could / to ˋpolish it with / the ˋmiddle of it / a ˋquarter of them / I ˋgave it to her / it's ˋnecessary / a ˋparty-member / we ˋhad to do it.

(Further examples of this kind of stress can be found in Exercise 67 on Intonation of Special Stress, and in the Appendix on Word-stress, Exercise 150.)

Exercise 9. Stress patterns

Note. See Exercise 3 for detailed instructions.

Key pattern: □□□□□

I ˈthink he ˋmight* / I ˈwant to ˋknow / to ˈdo it ˋwell / aˈnother ˋtime / it's ˈquite all ˋright / I ˈthink it ˋis* / he ˈthought he ˋcould* / I ˈthought it ˋwas* / she ˈtied it

ˋup / a ˈrubber ˋband / a ˈpiece of ˋstring / he ˈhad to ˋgo / it's ˈvery ˋgood / it's ˈhard to ˋsay / but ˈhurry ˋup / she ˈtook it ˋoff / they ˈput them ˋon / she's ˈmost upˋset / aˈnother ˋday / they ˈmustn't ˋknow / he ˈlocked the ˋdoor / it's ˈmuch too ˋbig / to ˈintroˋduce / a ˈwaste of ˋtime / they've ˈgone ˋaway / it's ˈall for ˋyou / he ˈwants to ˋlearn / I'd ˈlove to ˋhelp / a ˈglass of ˋwine / aˈcross the ˋroad / it's ˈnot for ˋsale.

* See note to Exercise 6.

Exercise 10. Stress patterns

Note. See Exercise 3 for detailed instructions.

Key pattern: □□□□□□

I ˈwanted to ˋknow / I ˈthink that he ˋmight / I'll ˈfinish it ˋnow / a ˈspoonful of ˋsalt / she ˈasked me to ˋgo / I ˈthought he had ˋgone / we ˈwanted to ˋsee / a ˈwalk in the ˋpark / a ˈplateful of ˋsoup / he ˈtold me he ˋwould / the ˈbest in the ˋclass / I'll ˈsee to it ˋnow / it's ˈwarmer inˋdoors / he ˈleft it outˋside / it ˈused to be ˋmine / a ˈhole in your ˋsock / he ˈborrowed a ˋpound / he ˈcan't pay it ˋback / she's ˈgone to the ˋshops / I've ˈfinished my ˋlunch / an ˈexcellent ˋmeal / in ˈspite of the ˋrain / the ˈhouse is for ˋsale / it ˈisn't alˋlowed / you ˈpromised to ˋwrite / she ˈwasn't gone ˋlong / he's ˈon his way ˋback / it's ˈstarted to ˋrain / he ˈdrank it all ˋup / the ˈengine won't ˋstart / I'm ˈsorry I ˋcame / I'm ˈglad you have ˋcome.

Exercise 11. Stress patterns

Note. See Exercise 3 for detailed instructions.

Key pattern: □□□□□

ˈfinishing toˋday / ˈdoing it aˋlone / ˈcarry it aˋway / ˈput it on the ˋfloor / ˈdirty underˋneath / ˈclean it with a ˋbrush / ˈtell me all you ˋknow / ˈfollow my adˋvice / ˈmind

how you be'have / ˈtry to do it 'now / ˈhalf of them have
'left / ˈget in touch at 'once / ˈsend them out to 'play /
ˈjust in time to 'see / ˈup above the 'clouds / ˈsitting all
a'lone / ˈwaiting for the 'train / ˈhoping that he'll 'come
/ ˈask him what he 'wants / ˈhave another 'cake / ˈhave
a ciga'rette / ˈwhat about a 'drink? / ˈbring along your
'friend / ˈcome and have a 'meal / ˈhow is Uncle 'George?
/ ˈwhy has no-one 'come? / ˈhang it up to 'dry / ˈlet me
take your 'hat / ˈput it on the 'shelf / ˈdon't be such a
'fool.

Exercise 12. Stress patterns

Note. See Exercise 3 for detailed instructions.

Key pattern: □□□□□□

I ˈthink it will be 'fine / I ˈwanted you to 'know / to
ˈfinish with it 'now / a ˈbucketful of 'ice / there ˈisn't any
'need / you ˈought to go to 'bed / the ˈhospital was
'bombed / he ˈwaited half an 'hour / you ˈonly have to
'try / I ˈnever have a 'cold / it ˈdoesn't make much 'sense
/ the ˈmiddle of the 'road / imˈpossible to 'say / beˈginning
with a 'ˈv' / we ˈthanked him very 'much / I ˈdidn't know
the 'way / the ˈbottom of the 'class / I'll ˈshow it to her
'then / we ˈpromise to be 'good / I'll ˈtry to be in 'time /
it's ˈdifficult to 'learn / he ˈdoesn't go to 'school / I've
ˈheard of it 'before / they've ˈcleared it all a'way / he's
ˈeaten all the 'cream / you're ˈwanted on the 'phone / I'll
ˈsee him in a 'week / he ˈborrowed half a 'crown / I
ˈhaven't any 'ink / it's ˈabsolutely 'true / so ˈdon't forget
to 'write / she ˈisn't on the 'phone / the ˈchildren are in
'bed.

Exercise 13. Stress patterns

Note. See Exercise 3 for detailed instructions.

Key pattern : □□□□□

I ˈthink he ˋwants to / I ˈwant to ˋmeet him / I ˈlike it ˋbetter / aˈnother ˋspoonful / I ˈthink he ˋought to / they ˈwant aˋnother / he's ˈplaying ˋfootball / you ˈmustn't ˋleave her / he ˈleft on ˋMonday / she ˈhas to ˋpractise / I'm ˈnot ofˋfended / perˈhaps they ˋdidn't / withˈout your ˋhat on / I ˈcouldn't ˋhelp it / we ˈnever ˋnoticed / you ˈneed a ˋhaircut / it ˈdoesn't ˋmatter / I'll ˈhave to ˋleave you / we'll ˈhave a ˋparty / it's ˈtime for ˋsupper / a ˈgreat ocˋcasion / a ˈpretty ˋpicture / acˈcentuˋation / he ˈhasn't ˋgot one / I ˈdon't beˋlieve you / we ˈleave toˋmorrow / an ˈawful ˋnuisance / she ˈwrote a ˋletter / a ˈglass of ˋcider / aˈnother ˋsandwich / ˈsuppose he ˋsaw me / a ˈstreak of lightning / a ˈclap of ˋthunder / a ˈpiece of ˋchocolate / a cup ofˋcocoa / she's ˈgone out ˋshopping.

Exercise 14. Stress patterns

Note. See Exercise 3 for detailed instructions.

Key pattern : □□□□□□□

he ˈstarted to ˋtalk to me / I ˈthink that he ˋwants us to / they've ˈpractised it ˋperfectly / perˈhaps you'll have ˋheard of it / she's ˈsewing the ˋbuttons on / some ˈcarrots and ˋcabbages / it's ˈquite inconˋceivable / reˈpeat it aˋgain for me / he ˈhasn't yet ˋpaid for it / she ˈwanted to ˋwrite to him / a ˈgallon of ˋparaffin / I'll ˈborrow aˋnother one / it ˈwasn't apˋpropriate / you'll ˈget it on ˋSaturday / they've ˈall gone on ˋholiday / it's ˈvery unˋfortunate / it's ˈnot the right ˋattitude / I ˈasked for it ˋspecially / a ˈletter from ˋGermany / I ˈdon't want to ˋfrighten her / she ˈwants a therˋmometer / it's ˈnot what I ˋasked you for / it ˈwants a new ˋbattery / they've ˈbought a new ˋwireless set / they've 'left Yugoˎslavia / a 'Beethoven ˎsymphony / we 'travelled by ˎaeroplane / he 'came on a ˎbicycle / it's 'just what I ˎthought it was / let's 'open the ˎother one / he's 'Shelley's conˎtemporary / I'll 'take it aˎway again / the 'clock on the ˎmantelpiece / the 'soup isn't ˎhot enough / the 'price has gone ˎup again.

Exercise 15. Stress patterns

Note. See Exercise 3 for detailed instructions.

Key pattern : □□□□□□□□□

I 'wanted you to ˎwrite about it / it's 'not the one I ˎborrowed from you / it's 'interesting [intrəstiŋ] to ˎread about it / I 'took it to a ˎwatch-repairer / she 'bought some new pyˎjamas for him / but 'where's the glass you're ˎdrinking out of? / perˎhaps you didn't realize ˎit / I 'think he did it ˎbeautifully / to 'satisfy the ˎschool inspector / they 'shouldn't need their ˎmackintoshes / I 'didn't think it ˎinteresting [intərestiŋ] / she 'doesn't want to ˎtalk about him / reˎmember what your ˎteacher tells you / you 'won't forget to ˎthank him for it / he 'needn't be so ˎrude about us / the 'doctor didn't ˎsee the patient / this 'isn't quite the ˎmoment for it / I'd 'like it with some ˎsoda-water / you'll 'need a rather ˎbigger saucepan / a 'teaspoonful of ˎsalad dressing.

Exercise 16. Stress patterns

Note. See Exercise 3 for detailed instructions.

Key pattern : □□□□□□

'show him up to his ˎroom / 'throw it into the ˎfire / 'walking along the ˎroad / 'that's to be left aˎlone / 'ready to go aˎway / 'standing behind the ˎdoor / 'why did you run aˎway? / 'tell her not to be ˎlate / 'sew it on to my

ˋcoat / ˈask them where they have ˋbeen / ˈshow me what you have ˋdone / ˈsing me another ˋsong / ˈwhat's the name of the ˋbook? / ˈmultiply it by ˋthree / ˈopposite the hoˋtel / ˈsuffering from a ˋcold / ˈbury it in the ˋground / ˈpolish it with a ˋcloth / ˈfill it up to the ˋtop / ˈfinish it if you ˋcan.

Exercise 17. Stress patterns

Note. See Exercise 3 for detailed instructions.

Key pattern: □□□□□□

I ˈthink he ˈwants to ˋgo / it's ˈnot the ˈone I ˋwant / it ˈisn't ˈquite the ˋsame / I ˈhaven't ˈbeen beˋfore / I ˈcan't beˈlieve it's ˋtrue / the ˈtrain is ˈvery ˋlate / he ˈhasn't ˈgot a ˋchance / I'm ˈsorry ˈI forˋgot / there ˈisn't ˋtime to ˋchange / a ˈletter ˈin the ˋpost / I ˈhope you ˈunderˋstand / on ˈFriday ˈafterˋnoon / they ˈplayed a ˈgame of ˋbridge / the ˈconcert ˈstarts at ˋeight / he ˈgoes to ˈwork on ˋfoot / he ˈtravels ˈhome by ˋtrain / I'm ˈsure my ˈhusband ˋknows / aˈfraid my ˈwife is ˋill / she ˈhas to ˈstay in ˋbed / the ˈfire is ˈnearly ˋout / it's ˈtime to ˈlight the ˋfire / I'd ˈlike a ˈpiece of ˋbread / it's ˈall the ˈsame to ˋme / exˈcuse my ˈbeing ˋlate / I ˈdidn't ˈknow the ˋway / the ˈroads are ˈvery ˋdark / I ˈcouldn't ˈsee the ˋhouse / perˈhaps you'd ˈcare to ˋwait / I'll ˈsee them ˈboth at ˋonce / it ˈdoesn't ˈmatter ˋmuch / I ˈcan't afˈford a ˋcar / he ˈpractised ˈevery ˋday / a ˈspoonful ˈevery ˋhour.

Exercise 18. Stress patterns

Note. See Exercise 3 for detailed instructions.

Key pattern: □□□□□□□□

I ˈthink that he ˈwants us to ˋgo / it ˈisn't the ˈsame as beˋfore / I ˈdidn't exˈpect to be ˋasked / we ˈshan't be in ˈtime for the ˋplay / you'd ˈbest be as ˈquick as you ˋcan

/ it ˈdoesn't much ˈmatter to ˋme / I've ˈwritten the ˈˈletter in ˋFrench / she's ˈgone for a ˈwalk in the ˋpark / it's ˈtime we were ˈhaving our ˋlunch / I've ˈtaken my ˈcoat to be ˋcleaned / the ˈoffice is ˈopen at ˋnine / this ˈshop doesn't ˈsell what I ˋwant / I'm ˈˈlooking for ˈpaper and ˋstring / this ˈenvelope ˈhasn't a ˋstamp / we ˈdon't want to ˈtrouble you ˋnow / aˈnother afˈfair for the poˋlice / you ˈshouldn't have ˈleft it to ˋher / she'll ˈnever reˈmember a ˋthing / she's ˈsure to forˈget what to ˋdo / perˈhaps you can ˈring her toˋnight / and ˈtell her to ˈleave it aˋlone / I ˈwanted to ˈmeet him aˋgain / he ˈpractises ˈonce in a ˋwhile / a ˈspoonful of ˈapricot ˋjam.

Exercise 19. Stress patterns

Note. See Exercise 3 for detailed instructions.

Key pattern : □□□□□□□□□□

I ˈthink it was an ˈexcellent afˋfair / I ˈwonder if he'll ˈask me in adˋvance / we ˈhaven't got an ˈenvelope to ˋmatch / the ˈoffice-boy will ˈshow you where to ˋgo / the ˈfactory is ˈworking day and ˋnight / the ˈlight should be in ˈquite another ˋplace / there ˈisn't really ˈquite enough for ˋtwo / I ˈdidn't want to ˈput him off aˋgain / I ˈdon't suppose you'll ˈunderstand my ˋpoint / the ˈbus is more conˈvenient than the ˋtram / the ˈconcert's being ˈbroadcast after ˋsix / it's ˈjust as good as ˈbeing in the ˋhall / we'll ˈswitch it on as ˈsoon as we've had ˋtea / I'd ˈˈlike a lump of ˈsugar in my ˋtea / I ˈshouldn't be surˈprised if they forˋgot / apˈproximately ˈten of you can ˋcome / the ˈothers must wait ˈhere a little ˋwhile / we'll ˈfetch you in a ˈcar in half an ˋhour / he ˈwanted me to ˈlisten to his ˋsong / we ˈfinished it the ˈday before he ˋcame / a ˈbasketful of ˈapples from the ˋshop.

Exercise 20. Stress patterns

Note. See Exercise 3 for detailed instructions.

Key pattern: ☐☐☐☐☐☐☐

I ˈthink he ˈwants to ˋgo there / we ˈought to ˈgive an ˋanswer / he's ˈnever ˈvery ˋpunctual / she ˈmarried ˈMary's ˋbrother / I ˈwant a ˈpound of ˋsugar / I'd ˈlike to ˈhave aˋnother / she's ˈcleaned the ˈkitchen ˋwindows / my ˈhusband ˈwants his ˋdinner / we ˈhad to ˈgo on ˋbusiness / I've ˈgot to ˈdo some ˋshopping / you ˈought to ˈbuy a ˋwireless / I'll ˈshow you ˈwhere to ˋput it / you ˈmustn't ˈwaste a ˋmoment / you're ˈlooking ˈsmart this ˋmorning / in ˈcase you're ˈlate for ˋdinner / with ˈno-one ˈthere to ˋhelp her / it's ˈtime we ˈwent to ˋdinner / a ˈdance toˈmorrow ˋevening / with ˈpeas and ˈbaked poˋtatoes / I ˈdidn't ˈwant to ˋlisten / he ˈdoesn't ˈspeak much ˋEnglish / it's ˈnot for ˈwant of ˋtrying / he ˈstudies ˈevery ˋevening / he ˈalways ˈdoes his ˋhomework.

Exercise 21. Stress patterns

Note. See Exercise 3 for detailed instructions.

Key pattern: ☐☐☐☐☐☐☐☐☐☐

I ˈthink that he ˈwants us to ˋtake him there / I ˈtold him to ˈwait in the ˋcorridor / now ˈwhat have I ˈdone with my ˋhandkerchief? / reˈmember to ˈget me aˋnother one / it's ˈcheaper to ˈgo to the ˋcinema / I ˈwonder if ˈDavid has ˋheard of it? / the ˈambulance ˈtook him to ˋhospital / apˈply for a ˈpost as a ˋlecturer / he ˈplayed us a ˈtune on the ˋgramophone / he ˈlooked for a ˈstick to deˋfend himself / I ˈought to have ˈsent her a ˋChristmas card / whenˈever you ˈcan you must ˋvisit us / Sepˈtember is ˈbest for a ˋholiday / you ˈmust have it ˈready by ˋSaturday / we've ˈhundreds of ˈplaces to ˋtake you to / I ˈwanted to ˈfinish my `library book / a ˈterrible ˈcold in the `head again / that's ˈnothing to ˈdo with the `argument / the ˈother boys ˈwouldn't a`gree with him / she ˈpromised to ˈcarry it `carefully.

Exercise 22. Stress patterns

Note. See Exercise 3 for detailed instructions.

Key pattern: ☐☐☐☐☐☐☐

ˈbuy her a pretty new `dress / ˈhoney and strawberry `jam / ˈwhen are you going a`way? / ˈwhat have you done with the `ink? / ˈhurrying off to the `train / ˈworking as hard as they `can / ˈprobably will in the `end / ˈcoming back home in a `bus / ˈtake it away to be `cleaned / ˈthat can be seen at a `glance / ˈwearing a funny old `hat / ˈgiving him a ciga`rette / ˈwhy have they left you a`lone? / ˈwhere have you hidden the `key? / ˈgo to another ho`tel / ˈnearly as far as the `bridge.

Exercise 23. Stress patterns

Note. See Exercise 3 for detailed instructions.

Key pattern: ☐☐☐☐☐☐☐☐

I ˈthink he ˈwants to ˈgo there `too / you ˈought to ˈknow the ˈway by `now / he ˈdid his ˈbest to ˈsave the `child / the ˈsnow was ˈfalling ˈthick and `fast / I ˈknow you ˈdidn't ˈmean to `hurt / that's ˈnot the ˈway to ˈfold a `coat / I ˈtold him ˈnot to ˈgo a`way / she ˈˈlooks a ˈlittle ˈpale to `me / he ˈhas to ˈgo to ˈwork at `eight / I ˈalways ˈlike a ˈcup of `tea / it's ˈtime the ˈchildren ˈwent to `bed / they ˈused to ˈgo to ˈbed at `six / a ˈglass of ˈbeer is ˈwhat I `need / he ˈleft the ˈroom withˈout a `word / he ˈused to ˈplay it ˈvery `well / I ˈsaw her ˈstanding ˈall a`lone / I ˈcan't forˈget the ˈthings he `said / they ˈsaid they ˈhad to ˈleave at `once / you'll ˈhave to ˈdo it ˈall a`gain.

Exercise 24. Stress patterns

Note. See Exercise 3 for detailed instructions.

Key pattern: □□□□□□□□□□□ . . . etc.

He ˈsays that he ˈwants us to ˈtake it aˋway / we ˈought to be ˈgrateful we ˈhaven't to ˋpay / you ˈknow that we ˈought to disˈcuss it toˋday / a ˈwoman has ˈfallen and ˈbroken her ˋleg / I ˈnever say ˈno to a ˈhot cup of ˋtea / then ˈturn to the ˈright at the ˈend of the ˋstreet / I ˈshouldn't have ˈthought he could ˈget here in ˋtime / he ˈtied up the ˈparcel and ˈtook it aˋway / the ˈgramophone ˈrecord has ˈbroken in ˋtwo / it ˈwon't be the ˈfirst time I've ˈgone without ˋlunch / exˈcuse my disˈturbing you ˈwhen you're so ˋtired / the ˈtram-stop is ˈjust a bit ˈfarther aˋlong / you ˈcouldn't have ˈcome at a ˈmore inconˈvenient ˋtime / it's ˈnot what I ˈwanted to ˈask you ˋabout / a ˈfriend of mine's ˈmarried a ˈgirl from aˋbroad / the ˈpaper and ˈink have been ˈput on your ˋdesk / I ˈsee he's forˈgotten to ˈleave his adˋdress / we ˈhaven't got ˈtime to arˈrange for it ˋnow / an ˈapple a ˈday keeps the ˈdoctor aˋway / the ˈbook you've just ˈlent me is ˈbetter than ˈmany I've ˋread / I ˈlike to sit ˈdown with a ˈgood cigaˈrette and a ˋbook.

Exercise 25. Plosives and rhythm

Note. Smooth rhythms of the type ♩ ♫♩ ♩ etc. are broken into the uneven rhythms of ♩ ♩.♪♩ ♩ etc. under the influence of certain combinations of plosives (p, b; t, d; k, g). When two or more plosives follow one another, only the last one is really "exploded" audibly, and the regular speech-flow is held back to allow the preceding plosives to be formed. This principle can be more easily understood by comparing words like **Friday** and **mi**d-**day**. The first 'd' of **midday** is not sounded, but the voice pauses slightly for it before uttering the second 'd'. A similar slight pause, with the suppression of the plosive, is often heard when a plosive precedes a **nasal** (m, n), an **affricate** (tʃ, dʒ; tr, dr), or a **fricative** (f, v; θ, ð; s, z; ʃ, ʒ). With this last group the plosive is usually less completely suppressed.

Read the following combinations, suppressing the plosive(s) in italics, but allowing time for its imaginary appearance. The teacher should read each group once, the student(s) repeating it three times after him.

chea*p* book / ri*p*e corn / ho*p*e to / ho*p*ed to / dus*t* bin / si*ck* baby / Sain*t* Paul's / bi*g* dog / bla*ck* dog / lam*p*-post / han*d*bag / to*p* branch / mea*t* tin / jum*p* down / Ham*p*ton / dam*p* cloth / to*p* girl / hel*p* mc / sto*p* now / dro*p* by drop / a sto*p*gap / ri*p*e cherries / to*p* drawer / car*d* trick / stee*p* track / dro*p* down / Thom*p*son / stam*p* these / a ri*p*e fig / gra*p*e vine / soa*p* bubble / ru*b* very hard / co*b* nut / ru*b* down / ti*p*-top / don'*t* talk / whi*t*e chalk / ru*b* gently / glo*b*e trotter / we*bb*ed toes / ru*bb*ed / ho*t* toast / si*t* down / we*t* ground / pos*t*-card / swee*t* fruit / le*t* me hel*p* them! / le*t* go! / mil*k* chocolate / a gol*d* nib / tha*t* German / the righ*t* thing / pu*t* tha*t* down! / a re*d* cover / a re*d* train / a goo*d* pudding / we ha*d* to / a ba*d* dog / a goo*d* girl / a san*d* pit / a pos*t*man / a goo*d* brother / har*d* times / col*d* meat /a lou*d* noise / goo*d* jam / a col*d* drink / an ol*d* friend / a goo*d* view / the Gran*d* Theatre / a sta*t*e theatre / I haven'*t* than*k*ed you / a ba*d* thing / now a*d*d them / eigh*t* pounds / in mi*d*-stream / we ma*d*e sure / loo*k* sharp! / qui*ck* march / no*t* now / a bla*ck* pig / ba*ck* to front / ta*k*e care! / a book-case / the ba*ck* garden / he dran*k* gin / he dran*k* nea*t* gin / we pi*ck*ed some flowers / a si*ck* child / we li*k*e jam / a boo*k*mark / a mo*ck* trial / to kno*ck* down / a lo*ck*ed door

/ a ca*k*e-dish / a dar*k* valley / ta*k*e this / ta*k*e tha*t* book /
ta*k*e three / a do*g*-collar / a lo*g* cabin / an e*gg*-cup / a bi*g*
girl / a pi*g*tail / fi*g* jam / a fo*g* si*g*nal.

Exercise 26. Plosives and rhythm

Note. See also Exercise 25, which practises the (partial) suppression of plosives. The presence of adjacent plosives in
phrases is mainly perceived through the changed rhythm,
caused by the pause made for the unexploded plosives.

*Read the following groups, giving adequate time to the
groups of suppressed plosives. The teacher reads each phrase
first, the student(s) repeating it three times after him.*

stop eating / sto*p* talking / he sto*pp*ed talking.
a pet hen / a pe*t* duck / a pe*ck*ed duck.
lock up! / lo*ck* doors! / lo*ck*ed doors.
a dry tea-cup / a whi*t*e tea-cup / a wi*p*ed tea-cup.
to knock out / kno*ck*ed out / kno*ck*ed down.
a hatter / an a*ct*or / a*ct* two.
to ask us / he as*k*ed us / he as*k*ed twice.
we hope it does / we ho*p*e to go / we ho*p*ed to go.
a stamp album / stam*p* paper / stam*p*ed paper.
stop him! / we sto*pp*ed once / we sto*pp*ed twice.
drop it! / I dro*pp*ed it / I dro*pp*ed two.
a docker / the shi*p* may do*ck* today / she do*ck*ed today.
tap once! / he ta*pp*ed again / he ta*pp*ed twice.
kick him! / ki*ck* Tom / he ki*ck*ed Tom.

Exercise 27. Plosives and rhythm (advanced practice)

Note. See also Exercises 25 and 26 on the (partial) suppression of
plosives. Here are longer phrases and sentences to practise
the characteristic pauses and uneven rhythm occasioned by
adjacent plosives. Be careful to make no pause in the general

flow of speech, particularly between the sounds linked by a
tie, viz.: ⌢. In longer sentences the sign ↑ is placed before a
convenient syllable for introducing a higher tone (see also
Exercise 50).

*Read the following, making adequate pause when forming
the suppressed plosives in italics. It may be necessary for the
teacher to divide up the longer sentences before reading them
in full.*

He ˈsto*pped* by a ˈlam*p*-pos*t* to ˈrea*d* theˆadˋdress.
I ˈcan'*t* ˋthin*k* today.
A ˈpos*t*car*d* toˆˈEnglan*d* ↑ ˈdoesn'*t* ˋcos*t* much.
He ˈsto*pped* to ˈwri*te* the ˋstree*t*-name.
I ˈpi*c*ked ˈnearly ↑ ˈeigh*t* ˈpoun*ds*ˆof ˈfrui*t* to ˈma*k*e ˋjam.
ˈTa*k*e care ˈno*t* toˆˈea*t* ↑ ˈtoo ˋmuchˆa*t* the party.
I ˈhel*ped* ˈtwo ˈdo*c*tors to ↑ ˈstar*t* their ˈcarˆafterˆit ha*d*
ˈsto*pped* ˋdea*d*.
He ˈpi*c*ked the ˈbes*t* ˈplums from the ↑ ˈto*p*mos*t* ˋbranches.
We'*d* ˈpi*c*ked ˈqui*te* the ˈbes*t* ˈpar*t* forˆourˋselves.
He ˈme*t* me a*t* ˈmi*d*ˈday to ↑ ˈta*k*e me ˈou*t* to ˋlunch.
ˈTha*t* ˈta*p* ˈdri*pped* ↑ ˈtwice as ˈfas*t* ˈtwo daysˆaˋgo.
He ˈcoo*k*ed ˈtwoˆˈeggs an*d* ↑ ˈpu*t* ˈtwo moreˆinˆan ↑ ˈegg-
cu*p* toˆˋea*t* them.

Exercise 28. Secondary stress and rhythm

Note. In any phrase or sentence the stressed syllables are not all
   given the same weight of emphasis. Some are less forcefully
   uttered than others, and the alternation of these groups of
   heavy and medium stresses helps to establish certain common
   rhythmic patterns. To understand the nature of this better,
   let us consider the main and secondary stresses of our example
   in the introductory remarks to this section on stress and rhythm.
   Here is that sentence, with its muscial counterpart in duple

rhythm. (The actual length of the notes is not of course quite so strict as suggested, but the alternation of the main and secondary beats of each bar approximates to the natural speech-stress.)

|Bert's |*friend* |John has |just |*bought* |two |*very* |fine |*old* |paintings.

$$\frac{2}{4} \; | \; \flat \; \flat \; | \; \flat. \; \flat \; | \; \flat \; \flat \; | \; \flat \; \flat \; | \; \flat \; \flat \; | \; \flat \; \flat \; |$$

The student is asked to note that the secondary stresses (in italics) cannot change places with the main stresses. A version which reverses the scheme and begins:

|*Bert's* |friend |*John* . . .
is simply not English. $\frac{2}{4} \; \flat \; | \; \flat \; \flat \; |$

For this reason it is most important to add bar-lines to a musical notation if it is used to show stress and rhythm. For example, the rhythm shown by $\quad$ can represent both

|**appetite** and **we are** |**wrong**;

but the former belongs clearly to the rhythmic pattern

$\frac{2}{4} \; | \; \flat \; \flat \; |$ while the latter must be shown as $\frac{2}{4} \; \flat \; | \; \flat \; \flat \; |$

The next eight exercises offer material for practising a few of the commoner rhythms of English speech and their parallel forms with the main and secondary stresses reversed.

Read the following groups, the teacher once and the student(s) three or four times after him. Try to keep the rhythmic pattern as steady as possible throughout the whole exercise.

Pattern: $\frac{2}{4} \; | \; \flat \; \flat \; |$

`appetite / `buy him one / `recipe / `heavily / `ordinary / `usual / `terrible / `talk about / `everyone / `terrify / `give

him it / `afterwards / `beautiful / `perfectly / `everywhere
/ `cauliflower / `pay for it / `think of it / `natural / `telephone
/ `answer me / `differ from / `offer them / `dinner-time
/ `send us one / `lend him it.

Exercise 29. Secondary stress and rhythm

Note: See Exercise 28. The same rhythmic figure now begins
with the weaker stress.

Pattern: $\frac{2}{4}$ ♪♪ | ♩ 𝄽 |

go a`way / in a `book / at a `glance / to my `friend / it is
`true / we are `wrong / what a `shame! / if you `please /
come a`gain / do it `now / lemo`nade / ciga`rette / as you
`like / can you `come? / out of `tune / cup of `tea / by
your`self / ten o``clock / half-a-`crown / every `day / not
at `all / later `on / do it `up! / put it `on! / fairly `cheap.

Exercise 30. Secondary stress and rhythm

Note: See Exercise 28. The same pattern is now shown in its
uneven form of ♪.♪ ♩   The extra initial length is most
clearly felt in the presence of suppressed plosives (see Exercises
25–27), but can also be caused by a long vowel or diphthong,
adjacent nasals and fricatives (or affricates), or even purely
subjective influences.

Pattern: $\frac{2}{4}$ | ♪.♪ ♩ |

`talk to him / `aptitude `practical / `amplify / `factual
/ (an) `empty one / `magnify / (it was) `sent to him /
`envelope / (a) `book to read / `octopus / `photograph
/ `wait a bit! / `show me one! / `that's enough / `educate
/ `afterwards / (some) `cake to eat / `thank them, please!
/ (he) `picked them all / (it) `must be true / (you) `ought to
know.

Exercise 31. Secondary stress and rhythm

Note. See Exercises 28 and 30.

Pattern: 𝄴

chapter ˋone / Doctor ˋBrown / up-to-ˋdate / let me ˋhelp / it's a ˋshame / (he) stepped aˋside / (he) asked the ˋway / (he) stopped to ˋask / what's the ˋtime? / what's it ˋfor? / ask them ˋnow / after ˋall / ginger ˋbeer / (it's) up to ˋyou / (you) can't come ˋin / afterˋnoon / eightpence ˋeach / up the ˋstreet / take them ˋall / put them ˋdown / (it) must be ˋtrue / (you) ought to ˋknow.

Exercise 32. Secondary stress and rhythm

Note. See Exercise 28.

Pattern: 𝄴 and

he ˋtook it from me / the ˋproper answer / aˋnother question / a ˋrailway engine / he ˋcan't have seen them / we ˋthought about you / some ˋchamber music / we ˋasked about them / a ˋshoe repairer / he's ˋlooking for them / I ˋnever knew that / you're ˋlate, as usual / he's ˋsure to blame me / you ˋwon't be made to / you ˋmust have known him / that's ˋnot the best way / I ˋbeg your pardon.

Exercise 33. Secondary stress and rhythm

Note. See Exercise 28.

Pattern: 𝄴 and

exˋamination / a ˈcup of ˋcocoa / apˈpreciaˋtion / he ˈwould'nt ˋask us / a ˋlack of ˋkindness / he ˈnever ˋgot there / a ˈclever ˋanswer / we'll ˈthink it ˋover / I'll ˈdo it ˋlater /

he's ˈnever ˎbeen there / a ˈpiece of ˎchocolate / he ˈdoesn't ˎwant to / I ˈshouldn't ˎthink so / I ˈalways ˎtry to / it's ˈnearly ˎmidnight / I ˈcouldn't ˎhelp it / it ˈdoesn't ˎmatter / a ˈpretty ˎpicture / a ˈtin of ˎgrapefruit / it's ˈnot the ˎfirst time / if ˈyou'll exˎcuse me / we ˈmustn't ˎblame them / you ˈought to ˎask him.

Exercise 34. Secondary stress and rhythm

Note. See Exercise 28.

Pattern : $\frac{6}{8}$ | ♩♩♩ ♩♩ | and | ♩.♩♩ ♩♩ |

ˎorder it for them / ˎlightning conductor / ˎsymphony concert / (a) ˎparachute jump / (a) ˎsewing-machine / (I'm) ˎthinking about them / (a) ˎfactory worker / (the) ˎdifference between them / surˎprised at his rudeness / reˎminded me of them / (a) ˎsecondary school / ˎdinner at eight / (we're) ˎtalking about you / (I'm) ˎwriting about it / (he's) ˎleaning against it.

Exercise 35. Secondary stress and rhythm

Note. See Exercise 28.

Pattern : $\frac{6}{8}$ ♩♩♩ | ♩♩♩ ♪ | and ♩.♩♩ | ♩♩♩ ♪ |

ˈdo it aˎgain / ˈtravel by ˎtrain / ˈup in the ˎbedroom / ˈover the ˎhills / ˈgive me a ˎpencil / (he) ˈtook us to ˎLondon / (I) ˈcouldn't beˎlieve it / ˈopen the ˎwindow / ˈwrite on the ˎblackboard / (we'll) ˈask a poˎliceman / ˈtelephone ˎlater / ˈnot before ˎeight / ˈhow is your ˎhusband? / ˈperfectly ˎwell / ˈthank you for ˎasking / ˈwhat is your ˎname? / ˈwrite it in ˎink / ˈsend them a ˎpostcard.

Final note

The foregoing eight sets of practice phrases show very briefly the changes that are possible in one rhythmic pattern by varying the positions of the secondary stress and main stress. It is, of course, possible for the stress to fall on any syllable of the rhythmic phrase. The following short series shows how the pattern ♪♪♩ ♩ changes from that of Exercise 34, namely $\frac{6}{8}$|♪♪♩ ♩ ↗| to that of Exercise 35, namely $\frac{6}{8}$ ♪♪♩ | ♩ ↗ by gradually shifting the stress.

ˋsecondary school |♪♪♩ ♩ ↗|

my ˋparachute   ♪|♪♪♩♪↗↗|

in a ˋmeadow   ♪♪|♪ ♩ ↯ ↗|

ˈdo it aˋgain   ♪♪♪ | ♩ ↗ ↯ ↗|

Exercise 36. Regularity of stress

Note. The examples given earlier of sentences containing many stressed words and others containing only few stressed words show that the apparent speed of utterance is largely dictated by the number of stressed syllables. The fewer the stresses, the more rapidly the voice skips over the intervening unstressed syllables. If we read any piece of prose at random so that we have a fair sample of mixed stressing, we find that the overall effect of this is to create the impression that stressed syllables occur at fairly regular intervals. When two or three stresses come close together, the speed of utterance is noticeably slower; when they are separated by several unstressed syllables, these syllables flow along more rapidly. The stressed syllables themselves move along at a much more regular speed. The following exercise has a gradually increasing number of unstressed syllables between the stresses. As their number increases, it may be necessary to slow down the speed of the stresses slightly, but care should be taken to read each new group at least three times in a steady and deliberate rhythm that is based on the stressed syllables. To facilitate reading, these stress-peaks will be printed in **bold type**.

The teacher reads each sentence once, the| student(s) repeating it at least three times at a steady, regular speed before the next is taken up:

1. You ˡ**came** to ˋ**see** him.
   You should ˡ**come** in order to ˋ**meet** him.
   You should have ˡ**come** before it got so ˋ**late**.

2. We ˡ**bought** a ˋ**book**.
   We have ˡ**bought** another ˋ**book**.
   We could have ˡ**bought** you another ˋ**book**.
   We ought to have ˡ**bought** ourselves another ˋ**book**.

3. It was ˡ**good** to ˋ**speak** to him about it.
   It would be ˡ**better** if you ˋ**spoke** to him about it.
   It would have been ˡ**better** if you had ˋ**spoken** to him about it.

4. I ˡ**can't** ˡ**come** ˋ**now**.
   I ˡ**could**n't ˡ**come** just ˋ**now**.
   I ˡ**could**n't have ˡ**come** beˋ**fore**.
   I ˡ**could**n't have ˡ**come** any ˋ**earl**ier.
   I ˡ**could**n't have apˡ**plied** before ˋ**yes**terday.
   I ˡ**should**n't have been able to apˡ**ply** any earlier than ˋ**yes**terday.

5. He ˈasked me to ˈgive him a ˈticket.
   He should ˈask if we could ˈgive him a ˈticket.
   He should ˈask us if we could ˈgive him another ˈticket.
   He ought to have ˈasked us if we could have ˈgiven him a few of the ˈtickets.

6. He ˈcan't ˈquite ˈread it.
   I ˈdoubt if ˈhe can ˈread it.
   I ˈdon't really ˈthink he can ˈread it.
   I'd ˈhardly have ˈthought he could ˈread it.
   I ˈshouldn't have thought it ˈpossible for him to ˈread it.

7. ˈTell her to ˈput it ˈdown.
   ˈTell the girl to ˈput it ˈdown.
   ˈTell the girl to ˈput the book ˈdown.
   ˈTell the girl to ˈput the book on the ˈtable.
   ˈTell the other girl to ˈput the book on the ˈtable.
   ˈTell the other girl to ˈput all the books on the ˈtable.

8. We'll ˈtell him to ˈclean it aˈgain.
   We'll ˈtell the boy to ˈclean the things aˈgain.
   You must ˈtell the young man to ˈclean all the things aˈgain.
   You should have ˈtold the two of them to ˈclean the whole bucketful aˈgain.

9. He ˈwrote the ˈletter on ˈMonday ˈmorning.
   He had ˈwritten all the ˈletters by ˈMonday afterˈnoon
   He could have ˈwritten nearly all the ˈletters by ˈnine o'clock on Monday ˈmorning.

10. He ˈcut the ˈbread with a ˈsharp ˈknife
    He ˈcut the loaf of ˈbread with a ˈsharp ˈknife.
    He ˈcut the loaf of ˈbread with a ˈbadly sharpened ˈknife.

He ˈcut the piece of ˈcloth with a ˈpair of ˋscissors
He ˈcut the piece of ˈcloth with a ˈsharp pair of ˋscissors.

He ˈcan't cut the piece of ˈcloth with a very ˈblunt pair of ˋscissors.

Exercise 37. Regularity of stress

Note. See Exercise 36. The following exercise consists of miscellaneous stress patterns to be practised as explained in the note to Exercise 3. The stressed syllables should in all cases be fairly regularly spaced out and the unstressed syllables be made to accommodate themselves to the steadier movement of the stresses. To facilitate reading, the stressed syllables will be printed in **bold type**.

The teacher reads a phrase, the student(s) repeating it after him at least three times consecutively in a steady rhythm:

I've ˈoften ˈwanted to ˋmeet you / ˈJohn ˈwanted to ˈtake it aˋway from her / I'm ˈsorry you ˈcan't ˋcome / we shall be ˈvery ˈpleased to ˋcome / we can ˈleave a little ˈnote if he ˈisn't ˋin / ˈwhat ˈname shall I ˋask for? / ˈsome peoˈple are ˈalways a ˈfew minutes ˋlate / he ˈcame ˈlate to the ˋoffice / we ˈtravelled all ˈnight in the ˋtrain / it's ˈnot ˈquite what I ˋwanted / ˈplease ˈcall back ˋlater / ˈwould you mind ˈcalling back ˋlater? / ˈplease help yourˈself to some ˋmore / there's ˈnone ˋleft / I ˈdon't ˈwant to / ˈevery ˈcloud has a ˈsilver ˋlining / I'm ˈnot very ˋwell today / I ˈthink he's feeling ˈbetter than he ˈdid ˋyesterday / we ˈshan't be ˋthere / we shall ˈsee you again ˈafter the ˋplay / I'm ˈnot ˈsure of the ˋnumber / it's ˈvery ˈkind of you to ˋask me / you can ˈalways ˈfind me at ˈthis adˋdress / it's ˈno ˈtrouble at ˋall / there's a ˈshorter way ˈthere across the ˋpark / ˈthat's the adˈdress you must ˋsend it to / ˈhave a cigaˋrette!

/ ˈplease ˈtry one of ˋmine / it's ˈnot ˈfar to ˈwalk if you ˈdon't want to ˈgo by ˋtram / ˈlet's ˈstart as ˈearly as we ˋcan.

Exercise 38. Unstressed pronouns

Note. Personal pronouns (we, you, him, it, etc.) and prop-words (one, ones, some, etc.) are normally without stress, even when they are at the end of a phrase. The next four exercises offer reading practice on this topic. Students should endeavour to place no stress at all on the pronouns, allowing them to form a single sound-unit with the preceding stressed syllable.

The teacher reads each of the following phrases once, the student(s) repeating it after him at least three times; the whole exercise should continue smoothly without a break as far as possible:

ˋcut it / ˋhelp me / ˋtell her / ˋask him / ˋbreak it / ˋmake one / ˋbuy some (sʌm, not səm)! / inˋvite them / ˋguard them [ðəm] / ˋwatch her / ˋstop him / ˋlock it / ˋcook some / ˋfeed him / ˋtake one / ˋpunish her / ˋsave some / ˋsend them / ˋget some / ˋmend it / ˋteach him / ˋvisit us / ˋfind them / ˋtry one / ˋeat it / ˋdrink some / ˋbend it.

Exercise 39. Unstressed pronouns

Note. See Exercise 38. The following exercise contains longer phrases, with the unstressed pronouns (in italics) in varying positions.

The teacher reads each of the following sentences once, the student(s) repeating it after him three times:

1. ˈGive *me* aˋnother *one*.
2. *I* ˈwant *her* to ˈshow *you* ˋround.
3. *She* ˈtold *him* ˈnot to ˈask *you* aˋgain.
4. ˈLet *me* ˈhelp *you* ˋdo *it*.
5. *I* ˈasked *her* to ˈtake *them* aˋway.
6. *She'll* ˈgive *you one* ˈnext time *you* ˋcome.

7. *I* ˈasked *her* to buy *me some* [sʌm] this ˋmorning.
8. *I* ˈknew *she* ˈhad *one* to ˋgive *you*.
9. *I* ˈsaw *him* ˋgive *you them*.
10. *He* inˈvited *us* to ˈgo and ˋsee *them*.
11. *He* ˈcaught *one* and ˋgave *me it*.
12. *She* ˈasked *him* to ˈfind *her* a ˋbigger *one*.
13. *I* ˈwanted *him* to ˈgive *you* a ˋnew *one*.
14. ˈGive *her one* if *she* ˋwants *it*.
15. Alˈlow *me* to ˋbuy *you some*.

Exercise 40. Unstressed pronouns (with adverbial particles)

Note. Verbs of the pattern "take off, push away, throw down" etc. take a stress on the adverb when the phrase ends with it. A pronoun preceding it is unstressed.

The teacher reads each phrase once, the student(s) repeating it three times after him. The unstressed pronouns are printed in italics.

ˈput *it* ˋon / ˈtake *them* ˋoff / ˈdo *it* ˋup / ˈlift *them* ˋdown / ˈshow *him* ˋout / ˈdrink *it* ˋup / ˈswitch *it* ˋon / ˈturn *it* ˋoff / ˈwake *them* ˋup / ˈread *it* ˋout / ˈput *it* ˋback / ˈeat *them* ˋup / ˈput *it* ˋdown / ˈcover *him* ˋup / ˈtake *them* aˋway / ˈlook *it* ˋthrough / ˈuse *them* ˋup.

Exercise 41. Unstressed pronouns (preposition and pronoun)

Note. The final combination "talk to him" etc. needs careful practice to acquire its characteristic rhythm. Both the preposition and the pronoun are normally unstressed, though there is a tendency to place a slightly heavier pulse on the **preposition**. This weak secondary stress is readily apparent if the final stressed syllable is gradually removed from the preposition + pronoun. In the examples:

ˋlook at it / ˋlooking at it / ˋwondering at it

there is already an appreciable but low-pitched stress on the third "at". It is also present, but to a lesser degree, in the other two examples. The pronoun "it" is completely unstressed. In this exercise, the pronouns (in italics) are always quite unstressed; the preposition may be given a very weak stress if joined closely to the pronoun, viz.: ˋlaugh at-*him*. If the three words are spoken as one close group, both the last words will be unstressed, viz.: ˋlaugh-*at-him*.

The teacher reads each phrase, the student(s) repeating it three times after him:

ˋthink of *it* / ˋgo to *him* / ˋlook at *them* / ˋask for *him* / ˋdream of *her* / ˋsit by *me* / ˋsleep on *it* / ˋrun up *it* / ˋargue with *them* / ˋwait for *me* / ˋwait on *her* / ˋlook for *him* / ˋwalk with *him* / ˋread to *her* / ˋcall for *them* / ˋcut with *it* / ˋtalk to *them* / ˋlaugh at *them* / ˋwish for *it* / ˋlisten to *me* / ˋwhisper to *her*.

Exercise 42. Unstressed pronouns (preposition and pronoun following the present participle)

Do the previous exercise again, reading it in the present participle form throughout, viz. ˋthinking of *it*, etc. Give the preposition a low secondary stress, but **do not stress the pronoun**.

Exercise 43. Unstressed pronouns (preposition between pronouns)

Note. See Exercise 41. A common final phrase is the group **verb + pronoun + preposition + pronoun**, e.g.

ˋtake it from her.

In this pattern the slight stress on the preposition is clearly felt, whereas the two pronouns are completely unstressed.

The teacher reads each phrase, the student(s) repeating it at least three times in a regular rhythm, making a slight but low-pitched secondary stress on the preposition:

ˋgive *it* to *me* / ˋhide *it* from *them* / ˋeat *some* with *me* / ˋbuy *them* for *them* / ˋstand *it* by *me* / ˋpin *it* on *him* / ˋlay *them* under *it* / ˋplace *it* over *him* / ˋlend *it* to *her* / ˋchoose *one* for *me* / ˋclean *it* for *me* / ˋread *it* with *me* / ˋbreak *it* for *her* / ˋcut *it* for *him* / ˋsteal *it* from *them* / ˋthrow *it* to *me* / ˋtake *it* to *him* / ˋtell *it* to *me* / ˋsell *it* to *me* / ˋkeep *them* for *me* / ˋplay *it* with *me* / ˋshow *it* to *her* / ˋopen *it* for *me* / ˋstudy *it* with *me* / ˋprac*tise them* with *her* / ˋhold *it* for *me* / ˋint*erview her* for *me*.

Exercise 44. Unstressed pronouns (miscellaneous)

Note. See Exercises 39-43. Longer phrases containing unstressed pronouns. The unstressed pronouns are printed in italics.

'fold *them* 'carefully and ˋgive *them* to *him* / 'take *them* aˋway from *them* / 'why didn't *you* ˋgive *it* to *him*? / I've 'told *him* I'll look ˋeverywhere for *them* / 'what can I ˋdo for *you*? / 'put *them* in my ˋcar for *me*, please / my 'father ˋbought *me them* / 'what did *he* ˋtell *you* about *us*? / ˋshow *them* to *them* / ˋshow *them them* / 'let *me* ˋsee *them* / 'where did *you* ˋsee *them*? / go 'up to *him* and ˋtell *him* about *it* / 'take *them* all aˋway with *you* 'let *me* ˋlook at *you* / 'take ˋcare of *her* for *me*, won't *you*? / 'I'll look ˋafter *them* for *you* / the as'sistant will 'wrap *it* ˋup for *you* / ˋread *it* to *him* / ˋwrite *it* for *them* / ˋspell *it* to *me* / ˋtell *me* about *it* / ˋshow *it* to *me* / ˋgive *it* to *him* / I 'bought *them* for *him* ˋyesterday / *they* ˋasked *us* about *it* / *he'll* 'sell *me* ˋtwo of *them* / *you* ˋprom*ised us them* / *he* 'doesn't 'want *us* to ˋsee *them*.

Final Notes on Stress and Rhythm

In a book that consists mainly of exercises on the more characteristic and normal forms of English speech, it is not possible to devote much space to exceptions to general rules and patterns. The statement made earlier that **content-words** are stressed and **form-words** remain unstressed (see notes preceding Exercise 1) is true in general, but one or two apparent exceptions are worth mentioning.

When a content-word is repeated within the same reference, it is normally **without stress** at its second appearance. Here are a few examples:

1. If the feet and hands are **warm**, the whole body will be *warm*.
2. **Love you**? Of course I *love you*!
3. They called the place **Beechwood**, though there wasn't a *beechwood* for miles.
4. "How many **dogs** did you see?" "Four *dogs*."
5. We can stand these **desks** on the other *desks*.
6. "Have some **wine**," said the March Hare.
   "I don't see any *wine*," remarked Alice.

But sometimes a feeling for rhythmic balance dictates a repetition of the stress, especially in sayings and proverbs.

ˈHandsome ˈis as ˈhandsome ˋdoes.

What's ˈsauce for the ˈgoose is ˈsauce for the ˋgander.

MORE and MOST

When used merely as form-words to make the comparative and superlative degrees of adjectives, they are usually without stress.

ˈYou're the *most* ˈbeautiful ˈgirl I've ever ˋmet.

The stress is kept when these words are adjectives or pronouns.

'Most of them 'speak 'English `well.
'Most 'small 'children ''like `toys.
'More 'haste, ''less `speed.

SOME

As part of the indefinite article (a, an, some) it is normally unstressed. As an adjective in contrast to OTHERS it is always stressed.

'Let me 'pour you 'out *some* `coffee. [səm] or [sm]
'**Some** people don't `like *coffee*. (Repetition of "coffee".) [sʌm]

(Note in this last sentence that "people" is also unstressed, because of an implied contrast with "other people.")

There is also an intermediate form of SOME, pronounced [sʌm] but with no stress. It is commonly found as an indefinite pronoun or with the not particularly common meaning of "one of a type."

`Take *some* for *me*.
'Let me 'pour *you* `out *some*.
'Find *some* 'English 'girl to `**prac**tise with.

STREET

Always without stress.

'Oxford `Circus; 'Oxford `Road; `Oxford *Street*.

PROP-WORDS

These are words standing for something that has already been mentioned or implied. They are unstressed.

'Please `take *one*. I 'asked for `red *ones*.
`**Some***one*, `**every***one*, `**every***body*, `**no**-*one*, etc.
'Let's 'talk *things* `**ov**er.
'That's `**my** *business*. It's 'no *business* of `**yours**.

REFLEXIVE PRONOUNS

These are without stress.

ᴵBuy *yourself* a ˋ**new** one. The ᴵchildren can unᴵdress *themselves* and ᴵput *themselves* to ˋ**bed**.

Important exception: ᴵPlease ᴵhelp yourˋ**self**! (when final only).

The same forms are used as emphatic pronouns, and with this meaning they have end-stress.

ᴵDo it yourˋ**self**. He ᴵasked me himˋ**self**. ᴵHe himᴵself ˋ**told** me.

WORD-STRESS

The problem of syllable-stress in longer words is outlined in Appendix II. The student will also find exercises and samples of words and phrases with Level Stress in the same section of the book.

INTONATION

Introductory remarks

By intonation is meant the "melody" of speech, the changing pitch of the voice. It is to a certain extent controlled by stress, for important changes of pitch occur only on stressed syllables. The remainder of the exercises in this book are designed to practise methodically all the commoner and unexceptional patterns occasioned by the rise and fall of the voice. Practically any phrase or sentence can be spoken in a number of ways, each carrying a different shade of meaning; consequently any given sentence appears in more than one set of exercises. A number of the subtler and more unusual patterns are omitted from this book as being refinements of simpler ones that have been included.

Broadly speaking, we can classify all the English intonation patterns under two types. Both types normally begin with the first stressed syllable fairly high, and fall step-wise from stress to stress until the last **significant** (meaningful) stress is reached. Type 1 then falls, remaining low for any further unstressed syllables; type 2 rises from a low tone, continuing the rise for any further unstressed syllables. An example of each of these main tunes will make this clear. In the graphic transcription between parallel lines representing the approximate upper and lower limits of the voice, the musical movement of the voice is shown by dashes (—) and dots (. . .), which stand for **stressed** and **unstressed** syllables respectively.

In the exercises the intonation is indicated by the following typographical devices:

ᴵhouse :	stressed syllable.
`house :	significant (final) stress; falling
‚house :	significant (final) stress; rising
but he :	unstressed initial syllables.

(Other symbols will be explained at their first occurrence.)

Examples.

Tune 1. *But he* ᴵdidn't ᴵsee me ᴵleave the `**house**.

Printed form : *But he* ᴵdidn't ᴵsee me ᴵleave the `**house**.

Tune 2. ᴵDid you ᴵsee me ᴵleave the ‚**house**?

Printed form : ᴵDid you ᴵsee me ᴵleave the ‚**house**?

Tune 1 (final fall) is used for definite remarks, orders, and question-word questions, and carries with it a sense of completion and finality.

Tune 2 (final rise) is used for other questions, all doubtful remarks, especially those with mental reservations, and carries with it a sense of incompletion.

The two types are capable of very great variety and many combinations, the most important of which can be practised methodically over the next eighty exercises or so.

Exercise 45. Tune I (one syllable only)

Pattern : `**No**

Repeat each of the following words three times on a falling intonation :

yes / look / pull / push / wait / stop / where? / why? / when?
/ here / there / don't / help / well / come / who? / which?
/ quick / oh! / hark! / speak / fine / good / write / start / sure
/ right / try / do! / next!

Exercise 46. Tune I (with introductory syllable)

Note. Introductory unstressed syllables are usually on a fairly
low tone.

Pattern: He's ˎgone

*Repeat each of the following phrases three times according to
the above pattern:*

we're ˎlate / *in* ˎtime / *they've* ˎcome / *at* ˎschool / *it's* ˎtrue
of ˎcourse / *from* ˎhome / *his* ˎname / *I* ˎknow / *just* ˎnow /
it's ˎmine / *at* ˎnight / *by* ˎday / *in* ˎtune / *up* ˎthere / *from*
ˎhere / *by* ˎnow / *he* ˎcan't / *he* ˎwon't / *from* ˎJohn / *we've*
ˎheard / *up* ˎhigh / *down* ˎlow / *you* ˎmust / *down* ˎtown / *on*
ˎtop / *by* ˎheart / *at* ˎsight / *in* ˎstep / *you're* ˎright / *they're*
ˎwrong / *at* ˎlast / *I* ˎwill / *as* ˎwell / *as* ˎyet / *in* ˎbed / *he's* ˎill
/ *a* ˎmatch / *the* ˎbox / *you* ˎsee / *her* ˎface / *in* ˎsight / *on* ˎfire.

Exercise 47. Tune I (two or three stresses, with intro-
duction)

Note. From the examples given before Exercise 45 we can see that
the voice descends step-wise on each stressed syllable. The
unstressed syllables between them are indicated as being at the
same level as the stress that immediately precedes them. They
may, however, move downwards towards the next lower stress,
and, in fact, usually do this if they are a large group. In excit-

able or enthusiastic speech they may even move upwards from the preceding stress, thus making a bigger leap down to the next stress. Here is a sentence to show the normal form and the two above-mentioned variants.

I'm sur|prised that you |haven't for`got`ten me.

1. (normal)

2. (unstressed falling)

3. (enthu- siastic)

The forms 2 and 3 are mentioned here for the sake of completeness but will not be specially practised. Stressed and unstressed syllables will be shown in horizontal steps as in 1 above and the variants ignored.

In exactly the same way a group of unstressed initial syllables may rise gradually to the first stress, as in second example above, but they will always be shown at a low pitch as in examples 1 and 3 above. It does not matter at all whether they are spoken at a level pitch or moving up to the first stress.

Read each of the following sentences three times :

we 'went for a 'ride in the `car` / *there are some* 'more 'books on the 'second `shelf` / *I must* 'get my `hair` cut / *we* 'haven't `time` / *you must* 'take him `home` / *I'll* 'come as 'soon as I `can` / 'help your`self`! / *we'll* 'meet you at the `station` / *I* 'like your 'new `hat` / *I shall* 'have to 'pump the `tyres` up / *my* 'wife 'smokes as much as `I` do / 'that's the 'best 'shop for `shoes` / *the* 'birds are 'singing in the `trees` / *he should have* 'asked 'how to `do` it / *they were* 'up before 'five o'`clock` this morning / *it would be* 'better to `leave` it / *we've been* 'trying to 'get in 'touch with you all `day` / *she will be* 'coming along

ˋlater / *you should have* 'told me ˋeverything / *it'll* 'soon be ˋspring / *we should have* 'left ˋearlier / *it* 'looks like ˋrain / 'let's ˡtouch with you all ˋday / *she will be* ˡcoming along ˋlater / *you should have* ˡtold me ˋeverything / *it'll* ˡsoon be ˋspring / *we should have* ˡleft ˋearlier / *it* ˡlooks like ˋrain / ˡlet's ˡgo for a little ˋwalk / *it would be* ˡbetter to ˡphone for the ˋdoctor / ˡmind you don't ˡmiss your ˋtrain / ˡboth the ˡchildren are ˡplaying outˋside / *we've been* ˡwalking through the ˋforest / *she is* ˡknitting a ˡgreen ˋpullover / *you had* ˡbetter ˡleave it till ˋlater.

Exercise 48. Tune I (question word questions)

Note. Questions beginning with what? why? when? who? how? etc. are normally spoken with a falling intonation (Tune I).

Pattern: ˡWhere did you ˡput my ˋhat?

— •   •   — •

⟍

The teacher reads each sentence, the student(s) repeating it three times after him.

'what's the ˋtime? / 'where have you ˋput it? / 'who would 'like some ˋchocolate? / 'what have they ˋdone? / 'why are you so ˋlate? / 'which do you 'like ˋbest? / 'when can you ˋcome? / 'who's ˋthere? / 'which is the ˋway? / 'what ˋday is it? / 'what's the ˋdate? / 'how ˋfar is it? / 'what have you ˋgot? / 'where ˋare you? / 'when do you have ˋdinner? / 'where does he ˋlive? / 'how can I ˋhelp you? / 'why ˋcan't you? / 'what's 'on at the ˋcinema? / 'what's the ˋmatter? / 'ˋwhich one? / 'how ˋmuch? / 'when did she ˋleave? / 'which is ˋyours? / 'how ˋare you? / 'what do you ˋwant? / 'who's coming ˋwith me? / 'when do the ˋshops open? / 'who is the ˋauthor? / 'where do you 'want to ˋsit? / 'why don't you ˋlisten? / 'what do you ˋwant me for?

Exercise 49. Tune I (miscellaneous longer examples)

Note. Revision of Exercises 45–48.

The teacher reads each sentence, the student(s) repeating it three times after him:

1. ˈGeorge plays ˈfootball every ˈSaturday afterˋ**noon**.
2. ˈWhat ˈtime does the ˈnight-train for ˋ**Glas**gow leave?
3. ˈHow ˈfar is it from ˈhere to ˋ**Lon**don?
4. ˈWhy didn't you ˈdo as I sugˋ**gest**ed?
5. *I should* ˈlike you to ˈcome imˈmediately ˈafter ˋ**tea**.
6. ˈWhere did you ˈsay you had ˈput my ˋ**glass**es?
7. *They* ˈwatched him reˈpairing the ˋ**wat**er-pipes.
8. *He* ˈpromised to ˈsend a ˈtelegram ˈon his arˋ**rival**.
9. ˈWhat is the ˈbest thing to ˋ**mend** it with?
10. ˈWhich is the ˈbest way to ˈget to the ˈstation from ˋ**here**?
11. *I* ˈwonder if I ˈought to ˈtake my ˋ**mack**intosh with me.
12. *We* ˈshan't be ˈable to ˈgo there aˈgain for a ˋ**long** time.
13. ˈWhere did you ˈbuy the ˈpretty ˋ**blue** one?
14. *It's about the* ˈworst ˈtime of the ˈyear ˙for ˈcatching ˋ**cold**.
15. *It's been a* ˈvery enˈjoyable ˈevening for ˋ**all** of us.

Exercise 50. Tune I (broken tune)

Note. With longer sentences, as in Exercise 49, it is not easy to let the voice descend throughout; it would get uncomfortably low if there were many stresses. To avoid this difficulty, and in general the monotony of a continuous descent, it is normal to raise the voice a little at any convenient stressed syllable and continue the descent from a new high tone. Syllables thus raised in pitch are given rather more importance thereby, an effect which produces a more lively impression than the same sentence spoken as a continuous descent. Compare the two following intonations.

We ˈmanaged to ˈcarry the ˈboxes as ˈfar as the ˈend of the ˋ**street.**

We ˈmanaged to ˈcarry the ˈboxes as ˈfar as the ˈend of the ˋ**street.**

The falling intonation is interrupted at "far" in the second example, though the voice does not rise so high as the first stress "man . . .". The first sentence sounds monotonous.

This "second start" in longer sentences will be shown in the exercises by a ↑ in front of the syllable to be lifted.

E.g. *We* ˈmanaged to ˈcarry the ˈboxes as ↑ ˈfar as the ˈend of the ˋ**street.**

In lively conversation these interruptions of the tune will be fairly frequent. If there is a strong feeling to exaggerate any part of a remark, the voice may even rise to a higher pitch than its initial stress. This purely emotional reaction does not, however, change the general pattern of the tune, which, in Type I, will have its final fall on the last stressed syllable as usual. Excited emphasis merely produces greater extremes of pitch.

In this exercise, however, we shall assume that we are raising the voice at the place indicated merely to avoid the monotony of a long descent step by step.

The teacher reads each sentence, the student(s) reading it twice after him:

1. *They* ˈmanaged to ˈcatch the ↑ ˈlast ˈbus into ˋ**town.**
2. ˈGeorge ˈplays ˈfootball ↑ ˈevery ˈSaturday afterˋ**noon.**
3. *We* ˈhope to ˈmove into our ↑ ˈnew ˈhouse beˈfore the ˋ**month** is out.
4. *I sup*ˈpose it ˈcouldn't ↑ ˈpossibly ˈhappen aˋ**gain.**

5. *The* ˈdoctor ˈordered a ↑ ˈtonic to be ˈtaken ↑ ˈthree times a ˈday after ˋ**meals**.

6. *I'm* ˈsorry I ˈcouldn't ↑ ˈquite make ˈout ˈwhat you were ˋ**saying**.

7. *She* ˈmust have ˈbeen on ↑ ˈholiday for ˈover a ˋ**week**..

8. *On* ˈEaster ˈSunday the ˈchurch was ↑ ˈmore ˈcrowded than ˋ**us**ual.

9. *The* ˈchildren ˈput on their ↑ ˈbest ˈdresses in ↑ ˈreadiness for the ˋ**birth**day party.

10. ˈWhere have you ˈput the (↑) ˈbox of ˈsweets that I ↑ ˈleft in the ˈbottom of the ˋ**cup**board.

11. *My* ˈhusband ˈalways ˈdoes the ↑ ˈwashing ˋ**up** for me.

12. *We* ˈwent for a ˈday's ˈwalk in the ˈforest in ↑ ˈspite of the ˋ**rain**.

13. *I'm* ˈreading a ˈmost ↑ ˈinteresting ˈbook by a ↑ ˈnew ˋ**writ**er just now.

14. *I* ˈhear ˈold Mrs. ˈBrown is ↑ ˈlaid up with ˋ**rheuma**tism again.

15. *You have* ˈnot ˈgiven me a satis ↑ ˈfactory expla ˈnation of your ↑ ˈstrange beˋ**hav**iour.

16. *It's a* ˈlong ˈtime since we've ˈhad such a ↑ ˈbad ˋ**thun**derstorm.

17. ˈMost of the ˈtime she was ↑ ˈtrying to ˈprove that she ˈhadn't gone ˈout of the ˋ**kit**chen.

18. *My* ˈeldest ˈdaughter has de ↑ ˈcided to ˈtake up ↑ ˈnursing as a caˋ**reer**.

19. *The* ˈmeadows at the ˈend of the ˈlane are ↑ ˈthick with ˈbuttercups and ˈdaisies ↑ ˈall the ˈsummer ˋ**long**.

20. *I have* ˈnever ˈseen such a ↑ ˈcrowd as there ˈwas ˋ**there**.

21. *You must be* ˈquick if you ˈwant to get your ↑ ˈshopping done in ˋ**time**.

22. ˈAll the ˈchildren from the ↑ ˈwhole ˈneighbourhood came ↑ ˈeagerly to ˈhelp ˈpick the ˋ**straw**berries.

23. *My* ˈfather ˈlikes to↑ ˈtake a little ˈnap im↑ ˈmediately ˈafter his ˋdinner.
24. *It would have been a* ˈgood iˈdea to have asked some ↑ ˈfriends ˈin to ↑ ˈcelebrate the ˈNew ˋYear.
25. *I* ˈwonder if I ˈought to ˈtake my↑ ˋ**mack**intosh with me?

Exercise 51. Tune I (repeated)

Note. The same principle is carried a stage further in sentences of co-ordinate clauses, or through the addition of non-defining relatives or other loose adjectival or adverbial phrases. Longer sentences of this type most naturally break themselves into smaller groups of Tune I.

Pattern:

She ˈgave him a ˋletter *and* ˈtold him to ˋ**post** it, *but* ˈnot

to be too ˋ**long** about it.

A vertical stroke will be used in the exercises to indicate the completion of any one intonation pattern, viz.:

She ˈgave him a ˋletter | *and* ˈtold him to ˋ**post** it, | *but* ˈnot to be too ˋ**long** about it.

The teacher reads each of the following sentences, the student(s) repeating it twice after him:

1. *They had* ˈdinner at a ˋ**rest**aurant | *and* ˈthen ˈwent to a ˋshow.
2. *It was* ˈvery ˋ**cold**, | *so she* ˈlit the ˈsitting-room ˋ**fire**.
3. *She* ˈsigned the ˋletter, | ˋ**fold**ed it, | *and* ˈput it in an ˋ**en**velope.

4. *I've* ˈjust ˈbeen into a ˈshop and bought a ˇ**watch,** |
   and ˈwalked out without ˇ**pay**ing for it.

4 (alt.) *I've* ˈjust ˈbeen into a ˈshop and↑ ˈbought a
   ˇ**watch,** | *and* ˈwalked ˈout without ˇ**pay**ing for it.

5. ˈCrowds of ˈpeople↑ ˈsoon ˈgathered in ˈfront of the
   ˇ**pal**ace | ˈcheering ˇ**loud**ly.

6. He ˈoffered her a cigaˈrette from the ˇ**box** | *and* ˇ**lit**
   it for her.

7. The ˈchildren ˈspent their ˈholiday in the ˇ**park** | *and*
   ˈdown by the ˇ**river.**

8. *I'll* ˈcome as ˈsoon as I ˇ**can,** | *so* ˈdon't ˇ**wait** for me.

9. The ˈmist ˇ**rose,** | *but it was* ˈstill too ˈdark to↑ ˈsee
   ˈdown into the ˇ**vall**ey.

10. The ˈgrocer ˈweighed the ˇ**but**ter, | ˈwrapped it ˇ**up,** |
    and ˈgave it to his ˇ**cust**omer.

11. The ˈengine ˈwouldn't ˇ**start,** | *so the* ˈdriver ˈlifted
    the ˈbonnet and↑ ˈlooked to ˈsee what was ˇ**wrong.**

12. *I'd like a* ˇ**long** drink, | ˈgin and ˇ**lime,** | *but* ˈnot ˈtoo
    much ˇ**gin,** please.

13. The ˈreferee ˈblew his ˇ**whist**le, | *and the* ˈgame
    ˇ**start**ed.

14. *I* ˈwent to the ˈcobbler's to↑ ˈfetch my ˇ**shoes,** | *but
    the* ˈdoor was ˇ**locked** | *so I* ˈcouldn't ˇ**get** them.

15. *He* ˈworks in an ˈoffice all ˇ**day** | *and* ˈspends his
    ˈevenings ˈstudying for a deˇ**gree.**

16. ˈTake the ˈfirst ˈturning on the ˇ**right,** | ˈkeep straight
    ˈon till you ˈcome to a ˇ**rail**way-bridge, | ˈthen take
    the ˈnext ˈturning on the ˇ**left.**

17. *You should eat* ˈmore ˈfruit and ˇ**vege**tables, | *but*
    ˈkeep off poˈtatoes and ˇ**bread.**

18. The ˈBoy ˈScouts ˈpitched their ˇ**tents** | *and* ˈlit a ˈfire
    to ˈcook their ˇ**dinn**er.

19. *She* ˈlaid the ˇ**table,** | ˈput the ˇ**kett**le on, | *and* ˈthen
    ˈcut the ˈbread for ˇ**tea.**

20. *You must* ˋ**wash** the cut, | ˈclean it with ˈantiˋ**sept**ic, | ˈthen ˈput a ˋ**plast**er over it.

21. *She* ˈhas her piˈano lesson↑ ˈtwice a ˋ**week,** | *on* ˈMondays and ˋ**Thurs**days.

22. *You've* ˈdone it ˈquite ˋ**well,** | ˈmuch ˈbetter than ˋ**last** time.

23. *It's a* ˈfilm for aˈdults ˋ**on**ly, | ˈnot ˈsuitable for ˋ**child**ren.

24. *We can* ˈmeet in my ˈoffice at ˋ**five** | *and* ˈtalk about it ˋ**there**.

25. *They were* ˈall ˈplanted in a ˋ**line,** | *like the* ˈrailings ˈround a ˋ**park**.

Exercise 52. Tune II

Note on the graphic transcription to be used.

In the notes preceding Exercise 45, the example given as a specimen of this second type of intonation was:

ˈDid you ˈsee me ˈleave the ˌ**house**?

This final rise on the word "house" is quite distinct, as the whole of it is felt on one syllable. It is, of course, only audible over the vowel-sound, but is still mentally present throughout the final "s". When the lowest point, at which the rise begins, comes on any non-final syllable, the subsequent syllables continue to rise to the end of the phrase and are mainly unstressed. If this lowest point begins on a comparatively long and open syllable, the upward movement of the voice is evident throughout. Read the following slowly:

ˈDid you ˈsee me ˈleave the ˌ**school**-room?

The rise on "school" is comparatively slight, and the leap to "room" more marked. A shorter, closed syllable in the same position would scarcely show a rise in itself at all, but as it is still subjectively a form of the same pattern with a clearly heard rising intonation through the final stressed syllable (such as "house"), the rise will always be shown graphically to begin on the last significant syllable itself. Viz. :

ᴵDid you ᴵsee me ᴵleave the ˌoffice?

Most transcriptions using a dot-dash system similar to that used in this book have shown the rise only when it occurs finally (. . . house? ‾╱). In other positions the stress has been shown low with any subsequent syllables rising (. . . office? ___ ·). We shall, however, show the rise of the second intonation pattern as starting on the last stressed syllable always, whether it is final or not. A similar sign will be used in the printed texts for practice, viz. :

ᴵDid you ᴵsee me ᴵleave the ˌhouse? . . . ˌschool-room?
. . . ˌoffice?

This will make intonation marking and the printed symbol uniform and also make the reading of the exercises both clearer and easier.

The following exercise practises the rise only, as in queries of one syllable.

Pattern: You? ‾╱

Read each of the following three times on a rising intonation beginning on a very low tone:

me? / him? / them? / all? / these? / those? / mine? / yours? / hers? / his? / theirs? / whose? / who? / when? / where? / four? / five?

Exercise 53. Tune II (single stress)

Note. See Exercise 52. As for examples of Tune I, the last significant stressed syllable will be printed in bold type throughout the exercises. The following exercise practises the rise over two or three syllables.

Pattern: ˌ**May** we?   ˌ**Could**n't he?

The teacher reads each phrase once, the student(s) repeating it at least three times after him:

ˌ**must** you? / ˌ**shall** I? / ˌ**does** he? / ˌ**will** they? / ˌ**ought** I to? / ˌ**should** we? / ˌ**should**n't I? / ˌ**is** it? / ˌ**isn't** it? / ˌ**were** they? / ˌ**wasn't** he? / ˌ**has** he? / ˌ**hasn't** he? / ˌ**do** they? / ˌ**will** he? / ˌ**could** it? / ˌ**have** you to? / ˌ**aren't** they? / ˌ**must**n't you? / ˌ**can't** we? / ˌ**shan't** I? / ˌ**was** it? / ˌ**does**n't she?

Exercise 54. Tune II (two stresses, final rise)

Note. See Exercise 52.

Pattern: ¹Can you ˌ**hear**?   ¹Will you be ˌ**in**?

The teacher reads each phrase, the student(s) repeating it three times after him:

¹have they ˌ**gone**? / ¹may I come ˌ**in**? / ¹is it ˌ**yours**? / ¹are you aˌ**fraid**? / ¹oughtn't we to ˌ**pay**? / ¹have you heard the ˌ**news**? / ¹are you on the ˌ**phone**? / ¹have you got eˌ**nough**? / ¹was it ˌ**you**? / ¹can you ˌ**see**? / ¹do you ˌ**know**? / ¹will you be ˌ**there**? / ¹did

he ˌgo? / 'were you in ˌtime? / 'are we ˌlate? / 'does it ˌwork?
/ 'have you ˌtime? / 'may I ˌtry? / 'was it all ˌright? / 'must
you ˌgo? / 'aren't you ˌwell? / 'couldn't you ˌask? / 'can I
ˌhelp? / 'would you like to ˌeat? / 'can you do it ˌnow?

Exercise 55. Tune II (two stresses, rise not final)

Note. See Exercise 52. It is a useful convention to show all the
syllables following the significant fall (of Tune I) or rise (of
Tune II) as unstressed syllables. Compare the following
examples.

You ˈspoke to him this ˋ**morn**ing.

ˈDid you ˈspeak to him this ˌ**morn**ing?

ˈDid you ˌ**speak** to him this morning?

The second question has "speak" for its last significant
syllable, and the rise continues through the rest of the sentence, shown as a series of unstressed syllables. In reality
"tails" of this kind are not entirely unstressed, for they always
retain a weak echo of their natural stress and rhythm. In this
example a weak secondary stress is still perceptible on "morning", but not strongly enough to need any special signs in either
marking or typography. The longer the "tail", the more distinctly
is the original stress and rhythm felt. (See Exercises 141 etc.)

Pattern: ˈWill you ˌ**tell** me?   ˈHave they ˌ**spoken** to you?

The teacher reads each question, the student(s) repeating it three times after him:

'are you ‚**ready**? / 'has he ‚**got** to? / 'can you ‚**man**age? / 'will you ‚**fetch** me one? / 'were you ‚**look**ing for me? / 'did he en‚**joy** it? / 'may I ‚**bor**row it? / 'can you ‚**make** one? / 'did you ‚**prom**ise to? / 'has she ‚**fin**ished with it? / 'does it ‚**mat**ter? / 'must you ‚**go** now? / 'did you ‚**ask** them? / 'is she ‚**like**ly to? / 'is it ‚**rain**ing? / 'did he ‚**vis**it her? / 'have they ‚**dam**aged it? / 'can I ‚**help** you? / *did* 'anyone ‚**tel**ephone? / 'have they ‚**eat**en them all? / 'shall we ‚**ask** him for it? / 'do you, ‚**like** it? / 'is ‚**tea** ready? / 'did the ‚**bell** ring? / 'was it the ‚**tel**ephone? / 'are we in‚**vit**ed? / 'are you‚**work**ing? / 'will you be ‚**free** in a minute or two? / 'have you ‚**answ**ered the letter? / 'will you be ‚**writ**ing to him about it?

Exercise 56. Tune II (many stresses)

Note. See Exercises 52–55. This exercise practises longer examples of the foregoing types. See Exercise 50 for the sign ↑ .

The teacher reads each question, the student(s) repeating it twice after him:

1. 'Did you 'have a 'good ‚**hol**iday?
2. 'Have you 'heard the 'latest ‚**news**?
3. 'Were you ‚**out** all day?
4. 'Has that 'letter been ‚**answ**ered?
5. 'Shall I 'bring some ↑ 'sandwiches for 'you, ‚**too**?
6. 'Is that ‚**your** little. girl?
7. 'Is it 'possible to 'get it ‚**out**?
8. 'Have you asked 'Mary and ‚**John** to come?
9. 'Shall I 'answer the ‚**door**?
10. *Will* 'someone 'meet you at the ‚**sta**tion?
11. 'Did you go a'way for ‚**East**er?
12. 'Would you 'like it 'painted ‚**red**?

13. ˈAre you ˈsure it can be ˌ**done**?
14. ˈCan you ˈcome to ˌ**lunch** tomorrow?
15. ˈMay I ˈuse your ˌ**phone**?
16. ˈDo you ˌ**us**ually work so late?
17. *Did* ˈanyone reˈmember to ↑ ˈlock the ˈfront ˌ**door**?
18. ˈAre these ˈsentences too ˌ**hard**?
19. *Did* ˈanybody ˌ**help** you with your homework?
20. ˈHas the ˌ**post**man come?
21. ˈCan you ˈbuy me a ˌ**news**paper while you're out?
22. ˈDo you like ˈreading in ˌ**bed**?
23. ˈDo you like ˌ**breakfast** in bed?
24. *Do* ˈyou like ˈbreakfast in ˈbed, ˌ**too**?
25. ˈIs it your ˌ**birth**day today?
26. ˈAre you ˌ**angry** with me?
27. ˈCan you ˈeat ˌ**more** than one?
28. ˈWould you ˈlike aˈnother ˈslice of ˌ**bread**?
29. ˈCan you ˈcome to the ˌ**pict**ures with me tonight?
30. ˈHave you got the ˈtickets for the ˌ**foot**ball match?
31. ˈMust we ˈbuy the ↑ ˈtickets ˌ**now**? (↑ is optional)
32. ˈMay I ˈwait ˈhere till they ˈcome ˌ**back**?
33. ˈDo you ˈmind if I ˈopen the ˌ**wind**ow?
34. ˈWill you be ˈstaying there ˌ**long**?
35. ˈAre you ˈgoing ˌ**camp**ing again this year?
36. ˈDid the ˈpostman ↑ ˈbring any ˌ**letters** today?
37. *Have you* ˈever ˈbeen in an ˌ**aero**plane?
38. ˈCan you ˈget it ˈmended by to,**mor**row?
39. *Can* ˈanybody ˈtell me the ˈname of the ↑ ˈyoung ˈman who was ˌ**speaking** to me just now?
40. ˈWere you in ˈtime for the ˌ**con**cert last night?

Exercise 57. Tune II (not questions)

Note. So far we have used only questions of the "yes-no" type as examples for Tune II. This tune is also used in its simple form for statements made as requests, for polite commands,

remarks of concern, sorrow, apology and almost any emotion
that makes an objective statement less definite. The following
exercise contains typical examples of Tune II that are not
"yes-no" questions.

*The teacher reads each phrase, the student(s) repeating it
two or three times after him:*

1. ˈThat's ˌ**right**.
2. ˈDon't ˌ**trouble**!
3. ˈPlease sit ˌ**down**!
4. ˈThat's ˌ**all**.
5. ˈDon't ˌ**leave**!
6. ˈIf you ˌ**like**.
7. *I'm* ˈso ˌ**sor**ry.
8. ˈDon't ˌ**move**!
9. ˈKeep on ˌ**try**ing!
10. ˈSee you ˌ**soon**!
11. ˈThat's ˌ**good**.
12. ˈPass the ˌ**salt**, please!
13. ˈThat's eˌ**nough**.
14. ˈDon't ˈhurt the ˌ**poor** thing!
15. ˈThat's ˌ**fun**ny.
16. ˈGoodˌ**bye**. ˈGood ˌ**morn**ing.
17. ˈIf they ˌ**want** to.
18. ˈO.ˌ**K**!
19. *It's* ˈall the ˌ**same**.
20. ˈDon't ˌ**both**er!
21. ˈThat's the ˌ**way**! (=that's how to do it)
22. *It's* ˈall ˌ**right**.
23. *I* ˈbeg your ˌ**pard**on?
24. ˈDon't forˈget to ˌ**write**.
25. ˈCome aˈgain ˌ**soon**.
26. *We* ˈshan't be ˈlong ˌ**now**.
27. ˈThat's the ˈone I ˌ**meant**.

28. *I* ˈhope you'll ˈlet me ˌ**know**.
29. ˈLet me ˈknow ˈhow you get ˌ**on**.
30. ˈDon't ˈgo aˌ**way**!

All the above sentences can be spoken in a more vivid form by using one of the patterns of special stress. The intonation given above is that of matter-of-fact and casual speech, not very forceful or lively.

(Examples of special stress begin at Exercise 64.)

Exercise 58. Tune II (not questions)

Note. See Exercise 57. A common variety of this has a few preliminary unstressed syllables leading straight to the rising tone itself.

Pattern:

A. *I ex*ˈpect he ˋ**knows.**

B. *I shouldn't be sur*ˌ**prised**

B's response is more casual, less interested, than *I* ˈshouldn't ˈbe surˌ**prised**.

The teacher reads each of the following, the student(s) repeating it twice or three times after him:

1. *I'm not sur*ˌ**prised**.
2. *I shouldn't have* ˌ**thought** *so.*
3. *It doesn't sur*ˌ**prise** *me.*
4. *It's what I ex*ˌ**pect**ed.
5. *You can if you* ˌ**want** *to.*
6. *That's* ˌ**right**.
7. *If you* ˌ**like**.
8. *I don't suppose it* ˌ**matt**ers.
9. *It's no business of* ˌ**yours**.
10. *You've finished* ˌ**earl**y *today.*

11. *I didn't* ,**see** *you there.*
12. *I didn't* ,**ask** *you to.*
13. *You can't expect anything* ,**bett**er.
14. *I don't suppose he* ,**cares**.
15. *It's all the same to* ,**me**.
16. *It's none of* ,**my** *business.*
17. *I hardly* ,**think** *so.*
18. *It isn't the* ,**first** *time.*
19. *It's not* ,**bad**.
20. *It's what she's* ,**paid** *for.*

Exercise 59. Tune II (varied significant stress)

Note. The significant stress is the one that takes the beginning of
the final fall or rise that marks it as Type I or Type II. The
choice of this syllable depends on the speaker's thoughts, for
by "significant" we are to understand the last syllable (or word)
that is of importance for the speaker's meaning. Thus the
most usual reading of No. 26 of Ex. 56 is

But the speaker may assume the anger, and be asking
either:

(a) is it *me* you are angry with? or
(b) is it *you* who are angry with me?

These would change the significant stress as follows:—

It is also possible to begin with this low stress, but
examples of this will be given in Exercise 79.

The teacher reads each question with the intonation turn as marked, the student(s) repeating it twice or three times after him:

1. ˈDo you ˈwant to ˈstay ˌ**here**?
     ˈDo you ˈwant to ˌ**stay** here?
          ˈDo you ˌ**want** to stay here?
               ˈDo ˌ**you** want to stay here?

2. ˈCan you ˈbreak an ˈapple in ˌ**two**?
          ˈCan you ˈbreak an ˌ**app**le in two?
               ˈCan you ˌ**break** an apple in two?
               ˈCan ˌ**you** break an apple in two?

3. ˈHave you ˈmet my ˈwife beˌ**fore**?
     ˈHave you ˈmet my ˌ**wife** before?
          ˈHave you ˈmet ˌ**my** wife before?
               ˈHave you ˌ**met** my wife before?
                    ˈHave ˌ**you** met my wife before?

4. ˈDo you ˈknow the ˈshortest ˌ**way**?
     ˈDo you ˈknow the ˌ**short**est way?
               ˈDo ˌ**you** know the shortest **way**?

5. ˈMust you ˈgo ˌ**now**?
     ˈMust you ˌ**go** now?
     ˈMust ˌ**you** go now?

6. ˈHas my ˈbook been ˌ**found**?
          ˈHas my ˌ**book** been found?
               ˈHas ˌ**my** book been found?

7. ˈCan you ˈcome to ˈlunch toˌ**day**?
          ˈCan you ˈcome to ˌ**lunch** today?
               ˈCan you ˌ**come** to lunch today?
                    ˈCan ˌ**you** come to lunch today?

8. |Will you |have a |little |more ,**meat**?
      |Will you |have a |little ,**more** meat?
        |Will you |have a ,**litt**le more meat?
          |Will you ,**have** a little more meat?
            |Will ,**you** have a little more
                              meat?

9. *Is* |Mary |going to |wear that ,**hat**?
      Is |Mary |going to |wear ,**that** hat?
        Is |Mary |going to ,**wear** that hat?
          |Is |Mary ,**go**ing to wear that hat?
            |Is ,**Mar**y going to wear that
                              hat?

10. |Can you |buy me a |second ,**copy**?
      |Can you |buy me a ,**sec**ond copy?
        |Can you buy ,**me** a second copy?
          |Can you ,**buy** me a second copy?
            |Can ,**you** buy me a second
                              copy?

Exercise 60. Tune II + Tune I

Note. Sentences beginning with a subsidiary clause or phrase
normally have Tune II for this introductory part, followed by
Tune I for the main clause.

|When he ,**came**, | *I* |asked him to ‘**wait**

If there is no sense-pause made between the two parts of such
a sentence, as may often happen with shorter phrases not followed in print by a comma, the whole sentence may be spoken
as one group with Tune I only.

|After the ,**game** | *we* |had some ,**tea**.

ˡAfter the ˡgame we ˡhad some ˋtea.

——　·　·　——　·　——　·　　　＼

The teacher reads each of the following (in two sense-groups as indicated), the student(s) repeating it twice after him:

1. ˡWhen he ˌsaw us, | he ˡran aˋway.
2. ˡSince you reˡfuse to ˌhelp, | I *must* ˡdo it aˋlone.
3. ˡJust as the ˡtrain was ˌstarting, | he ˡjumped ˋin.
4. *When*ˡever I ˡhave a ˌheadache, | *I* ˡtake a ˡcup of ˡstrong ˋtea.
5. ˡIf you ˌlike, | *I'll* ˡsend the ˋcar for you.
6. ˡAs she was ˡcoming down the ˌstairs, | her ˋfoot slipped.
7. ˡAfter we've ˡhad our ˌdinner, | *we can* ˡsit in the ˋgarden.
8. *In* ˡspite of the ˌrain, | *they* ˡall ˡcame as they had ˋpromised.
9. *Al*ˡthough your ˡwork ↑ ˡstill ˡhas some misˌtakes, | *it is* ˡbetter than beˋfore.
10. *Be*ˡfore I had ˡtime to ↑ ˡopen the ˌdoor, | he ˡknocked aˋgain.
11. *Using* ˡall his ˌstrength, | *he aimed a ter*ˡrific ˡblow at his opˋponent.
12. *Un*ˡless it ˡrains in the ˡnext few ˌdays, | *we shall have a* ˡvery ˡpoor ˋharvest.
13. *Sinc*e ˡearly ˌmorning | *I have been pre*ˡparing for the ˋparty.
14. ˡSo ˡhard did he ˌwork, | *that he was* ˡquite worn ˋout.
15. *After* ˡall I've ˡdone for my ˌchildren, | *they* ˡsimply ˡgo and ˋleave me.
16. ˡWhat he ˌmeant by it, | *I* ˡcannot iˋmagine.
17. ˡIf there's ˌtime, | *we can* ˡhave a ˡgame of ↑ ˡtennis ˡafter our ˋbathe.

18. ˈSince her ˌillness | *she has* ˈnever ˈreally ˈˈlooked ˋ**well**.

19. *Be*ˈfore you ˌ**go**, | ˈhave a ˈˈlook at my ˈlatest ˋ**photos**.

20. *Be*ˈfore he ˈknew what was ˌ**hap**pening, | *the* ˈcar ˈskidded and ↑ ˈmounted the ˋ**pave**ment.

21. ˈAfter ˌ**all**, | *you've* ˈstill got aˈnother ˋ**chance**.

22. *With* ˈfierce determiˌ**nat**ion, | *he* ˈrowed toˈwards the ˈdrowning ˋ**girl**.

23. *Be*ˈneath the ˈshade of a ˌ**tree** | *was a* ˈgarden ˋ**seat**.

24. ˈPushing with ˈboth ˌ**hands**, | *she* ˈtried to ˈfree herself from his ˋ**grasp**.

25. *On the* ˈstroke of ˌ**mid**night | *they* ˈall ˈraised their ˈglasses to ↑ ˈdrink to the ˈNew ˋ**Year**.

26. ˈBarking exˌ**cit**edly, | *the* ˈdog ˈrushed ˈout to the ˈgarden ˋ**gate**.

27. *Al*ˈthough she was ˈvery ˌ**poor**, | *she was* exˈtremely ˋ**hon**est.

28. ˈWhen the ˈwinter is ˌ**over**, | *we must* ˈhave the ˈhouse ˋ**paint**ed.

29. *On the* ˈtop of a ˌ**hill** | *stood an* ˈold ˋ**church**.

30. *On the* ˈbottom ˌ**shelf** | *you'll* ˈfind a ˈblue ˋ**book**.

31. *With*ˈout ˈknowing what she was ˌ**do**ing, | *she be*ˈgan to ˋ**run**.

32. ˈWhen you're ˈquite ˌ**rea**dy, | ˈwe can ˋ**go**.

33. *Be*ˈfore you ˈtell us any ˌ**more**, | *you* ˈmust have ˈsomething to ˋ**eat**.

34. *If it's* ˈall the ˈsame to ˌ**you**, | *I'd* ˈrather ˋ**walk**.

35. ˈHolding the ˈkey in ˈone ˌ**hand**, | *he* ˈfelt for the ˈkeyhole with the ˋ**oth**er.

Exercise 61. Tune I + Tune II

Note. This is the usual pattern for a sentence where the main clause is followed by a clause or phrase that strongly qualifies it. It is particularly common with conditions spoken in a hesitant manner.

Pattern: I ˈeat ˋsteak, | *when I can* ˌget *it.*

Notice that the Tune II section is commonly without any stresses before the significant one when used (as here) for final qualifying clauses or phrases.

The teacher reads each sentence, the student(s) repeating it twice after him. Make an appreciable pause at the bar-line of each sentence.

1. *I* preˈfer ˋred, | *if you've* ˌgot *it.*
2. *We can* ˋwalk *there* | *if there's* ˌtime.
3. ˈI'd ˈlike some, ˋtoo, | *if you can* ˌfind *any.*
4. *I should* ˈlike to ˋread *it,* | *when you've* ˌfinished with *it.*
5. *There'll be* ˈnothing ˋleft, | *after you've had* ˌyours.
6. *You'll be* ˋlate | *if you don't hurry* ˌup.
7. *I'd* ˈbuy a ˋnew *one,* | *if I could af*ˌford *it.*
8. *They'll* ˈhave to ˈcross by ˋboat | *until the* ˌbridge *is built.*
9. *We must* ˈput ˋup *with it,* | *since it can't be* ˌhelped.
10. *You'll be* ˈdead ˋtired | *before the* ˌday's *out.*
11. *I* ˈdon't underˋstand *you* | *when you speak so* ˌfast.
12. *We* ˈdidn't ˈsee the beˋginning, | *being so* ˌlate.
13. *It's* ˈno use ˋgoing | *until the* ˌlibrary's *open.*
14. ˈEveryone beˋlieved *it* | *at the time when I* ˌspoke *to you.*
15. *I* ˈalways ˈclean my ˋteeth | *after* ˌeating.
16. ˈI ˈthink she is unˋkind, | *since you* ˌask *me.*
17. ˈLet's swim ˈout to that ˋrock, | *if it's not too* ˌfar.
18. *I* ˈcan't underˈstand ↑ ˈwhy there's ˈno ˋanswer, | *unless this is the wrong* ˌhouse.
19. *We must* ˈdo as he ˋsays, | *since there's no* ˌother *way.*
20. *That's* ˈquite ˋright, | *as far as* ˌI *know.*

The intonation pattern of this exercise and the next one should be compared with the type introduced in Exercise 128, where a similar pattern occurs as a single unit.

Exercise 62. Tune I + Tune II

Note. The pattern of Exercise 61 is also used in a very similar type of sentence where a remark is followed by a short phrase that qualifies it, rather in the manner of an afterthought. The speaker makes a remark, hesitates, then adds a phrase to make it less definite. This phrase will be heard as a rising intonation (Tune II).

Pattern: *I'll* ˈask him myˈself, | *if* ˌnecessary.

The teacher reads each sentence, the student(s) repeating it twice after him. Make an appreciable pause at the bar-line of each sentence.

1. ˈThat's the ˈlast, | *I* ˌthink.
2. *He's* ˈlate, | *as* ˌusual.
3. *I* ˈthink it's ˈquite ˈfair, | *on the* ˌwhole.
4. *We were* ˈalways ˈgood ˈfriends, | *till last* ˌyear.
5. ˈNothing can ˈsave her ˈnow, | *except a* ˌmiracle.
6. *I* ˈcan't ˈdo it | *just at the* ˌmoment.
7. *She* ‖lunches ˈearly, | ˌusually.
8. *It'll be* ˈready in a ˈmoment, | *if you'll* ˌwait.
9. *I'll* ˈdo it at ˈonce | *if* ˌneed be.
10. ˈHe was ˈright, | *neverthe*ˌless.
11. ˈThey knew ˈnothing aˈbout it, | *till* ˌnow.
12. *She's* ˈvery hard-ˈworking, | *on the* ˌother hand.
13. *In* spring it ˈrains a ˈlot, | ˌgenerally.
14. *She* ˈdoes ˈwhat she's ˈtold, | *of* ˌcourse.
15. ˈBaby ˈcries ↑ ˈevery ˈnight, | *from* ˌmy experience.
16. *We have* ˈvery little ˈsnow here | *as a* ˌrule.

17. *They would* ˈlike ˈsomething to ˋeat, | *I* iˌmagine.
18. *I'll* ˈdo it ˋnow, | *if there's* ˌtime.
19. *We* ˈhaven't much ˋmoney left, | ˌmind you.
20. ˈNor have ˋwe, | *as a matter of* ˌfact.

Exercise 63. Tune I (replacing I + II)

Note. The two previous exercises deal with a statement followed
by a clause or shorter phrase qualifying it as an afterthought.
If the speaker consciously incorporates this afterthought into
the idea he wishes to express, there will be no pause and the
whole statement reverts to the normal factual and objective
Tune I. This sometimes needs a different word-order.

Pattern: 1. *I'll* ˋask him | *when he* ˌcalls.   (as an
afterthought)

2. *I'll* ˈask him ˈwhen he ˋcalls. (as one idea)

Read the following sentences from Exercise 61 *and* 62 *in
the two ways suggested. The teacher reads each sentence, the
student(s) repeating it twice after him: the variant reading of
each sentence should be done by the same student(s).*

1. *You'll be* ˈdead ˋtired | *before the* ˌday's out.
   You'll be ˈdead ˈtired before the ˋday's out.
2. *You'll be* ˋlate | *if you don't hurry* ˌup.
   You'll be ˈlate if you ˈdon't hurry ˋup.
3. *I'd* ˈbuy a ˋnew one | *if I could af*ˌford it.
   I'd ˈbuy a ˈnew one if I could afˋford it.
4. *It's* ˈno use ˋgoing | *until the* ˌlibrary's open.
   It's ˈno use ˈgoing until the ˋlibrary's open.
5. *That's* ˈquite ˋright, | *as far as* ˌI know.
   That's ˈquite ˈright as far as ↑ˋI know.

6. *I* ˈthink it's ˈquite ˋfair, | *on the* ˏwhole.
   I ˈthink on the ˈwhole it's quite ˋfair.

7. ˈNothing can ˈsave her ˋnow, | *except a* ˏmiracle.
   ˈNothing can ˈsave her ˈnow except a ↑ˋmiracle.

8. *I* ˈcan't ˋdo it | *just at the* ˏmoment.
   I ˈcan't ˈdo it ˈjust at the ˋmoment.

9. *She* ˈlunches ˋearly, | ˏusually.
   She ˈusually ˈlunches ˋearly.

10. ˈHe was ˋright, | *neverthe*ˏless.
    ˈNevertheˈless he was ˋright.

11. ˈThey knew ˈnothing aˋbout it, | *till* ˏnow.
    ˈThey knew ˈnothing aˈbout it till ˋnow.

12. *In* ˈspring it ˈrains a ˋlot, | ˏgenerally.
    In ˈspring it ˈgenerally ˋrains a lot.

13. *We have* ˈvery little ˋsnow here, | *as a* ˏrule.
    As a ˈrule we have ˈvery little ˋsnow here.

14. *They would* ˈlike ˈsomething to ˋeat, | *I i*ˏmagine.
    *I i*ˈmagine they would ˈlike ˈsomething to ˋeat.

15. *I'll* ˈdo it ˋnow, | *if there's* ˏtime.
    I'll ˈdo it ˈnow if there's ˋtime.

Exercise 64. Special Stress (stress for meaning)

Note. Apart from the obvious habit of exaggerating the movement
of the voice when emotionally excited, there is the very important English speech habit of emphasizing one or two words in
a sentence to give special point to the speaker's ideas. When
this is done in simple objective statements, the word (or
syllable) to be made prominent is spoken with a falling intonation, starting higher than the previous stress. Syllables to be
spoken in this way will appear in the exercises in CAPITALS
to distinguish them from the usual significant intonation turn
in heavy type. (The first person singular, as it is always a
capital letter, will appear in heavy type when it takes this
special stress: **I**.)

Pattern:

1. (normal) *He* ˈwants me to ˋ**stay.**

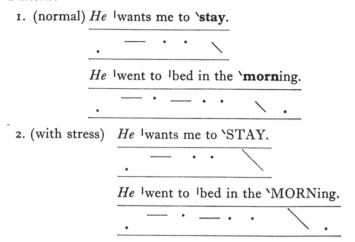

He ˈwent to ˈbed in the ˋ**morn**ing.

2. (with stress) *He* ˈwants me to ˋSTAY.

He ˈwent to ˈbed in the ˋMORNing.

He ˈwants me to ˋSTAY (though I intended to leave).

He ˈwent to ˈbed in the ˋMORNing (instead of at night, as you might expect).

Students should note that the prominence given to such syllables depends for its effect more on the characteristic big leap down than on a stonger stress. The force with which the syllable is spoken need be no stronger than the normal pattern, where no idea is to be made especially prominent.

The teacher reads each of the following sentences with special prominence given to the last word, the student(s) repeating it twice or three times after him:

ˈthese ˈgoods are for ˋEXport / *you're* ˈnearly ˈfalling aˋSLEEP / *they* ˈstayed until ˋMIDnight / *I* ˈdidn't ˈknow you were ˋHERE / *he* ˈeats ˈham with ˋMARmalade / *he* ˈrode his ˈhorse up the ˋSTAIRS / *I* ˈcouldn't say ˈno to ˋYOU / *she* ˈwashes her ˈface in ˋMILK / *we* ˈhaven't

ˈseen him for ˈYEARS / *you* ˈlook as ˈif you're ˈANGry / *he* ˈpays me ˈfor it ˈWEEKly / *you* ˈwon't ˈlisten to ˈANybody / ˈmother ˈdidn't ˈsay a ˈWORD / *I've* finished the ˈwashing, ˈTOO / *he* ˈworks at ˈNIGHT / *it's* ˈmore than ˈI can afˈFORD / *his* ˈfavourite ˈgame is ˈFOOTball / *she* ˈkeeps it ˈin her ˈPOCKet / *we* ˈused to ˈhave a ˈgarden ˈon the ˈROOF / *I* ˈdoubt if ˈhe'll aˈGREE / *they* ˈwalked from ˈLondon to ˈGLASgow / *in* ˈsome ˈcountries ˈwomen ˈwear ˈTROUSers / *she's* ˈlearnt it ˈall by ˈHEART / *she's* ˈleaving toˈmorrow by ˈAIR / *you should have* ˈcome ˈEARlier / *it* ˈlooks like ˈRAIN / *we* ˈought to have ˈpaid him ˈYESterday / *I* ˈcut myself on a ˈpiece of ˈPAper / *he* ˈdid it ˈall for ˈNOthing / *I* ˈthought you ˈasked for ˈTEA.

Exercise 65. Special Stress (Tune I)

Note. See Exercise 64. Even greater prominence is given to one idea by giving it the wide leap we have just practised, and at the same time leaving **all** other syllables unstressed.

Patterns: Tune I with special stress (see previous exercise), is given added force in the form:

He wants me to ˈSTAY.

The above will be the standard way of showing and printing this pattern in this book, but students should notice two slight variations that are commonly used instead of it.

1. The syllables marked as unstressed normally retain a shadow of their normal stresses, which are, however, very much reduced and on a fairly low tone.

He wants me to ˈSTAY.

2. The syllables preceding the special stress are sometimes heard to rise slightly on their way to the high jump of the specially stressed syllable; they may sound completely unstressed, or again, as at 1 above, a weak echo of the original stressing may be perceived through the rhythm.

2a. *He wants me to* `STAY.    **2b.** *He wants me to* `STAY.

It is quite immaterial which pattern is used. The tendency for the voice to rise towards the special stress is more usual when this introductory unstressed group is rather long.

The teacher reads the following sentences unstressed, with special stress on the last word, the student(s) repeating it two or three times after him:

I don't think I `CAN | *I cooked it my*`SELF | *I told you to leave it a*`LONE | *it'll be ready to*`DAY | *we couldn't understand a* `WORD | *I don't believe it's* `POSSible | *he wants it at* `ONCE | *she was simply* `FURious | *the water was* `BOILing | *it has rained for a* `MONTH | *it was all a mis*`TAKE | *he was bitten by a* `DOG | *he's done it a*`GAIN | *they did what they* `COULD | *you can't go out like* `THAT | *he fell ill on his* `BIRTHday | *I'll ring the bell till he* `ANSwers | *it would be better to* `PHONE | *you must do as you're* `TOLD | *they're going to live in a* `CARavan | *I'm told she's his* `WIFE | *he's having a holiday in* `ROME | *it's always better to* `WAIT | *this calendar is for nineteen-*`FIFty | *this isn't the one I* `ASKED for.*

Exercise 66. Special Stress (Tune I)

Note. See Exercises 64 and 65. Here are some of the previous sentences with the normal stresses given back to the introductory unstressed sections.

The teacher reads each sentence as shown, the student(s) repeating it twice or three times after him:

I ˈdon't ˈthink I ˋCAN / *I* ˈtold you to ˈleave it aˋLONE / *we* ˈcouldn't underˈstand a ˋWORD / *he was* ˈbadly ˈbitten by a ˋDOG / *I* ˈdon't beˈlieve it's ˋPOSSible / *they* ˈdid ˈwhat they ˋCOULD / *you* ˈcan't go ˈout like ˋTHAT / *he* ˈfell ˈill on his ˋBIRTHday / *I'll* ˈring the ˈbell till he ˋANSwers / *they're* ˈgoing to ˈlive in a ˋCARavan / *I'm* ˈtold she's his ˋWIFE / *he's* ˈhaving a ˈholiday in ˋROME / *it's* ˈalways ˈbetter to ˋWAIT / *this* ˈisn't the ˈone I ˋASKED for.

Exercise 67. Special Stress (Tune I)

Note. See Exercise 64-66. In this exercise the special stress is not necessarily at the end. All the other syllables will be in the unstressed form.

Pattern: *He wants* ˋME *to stay.*   ˋHE *wants me to stay.*

He wants ˋME *to stay* (I'm the one who has been asked).

ˋHE *wants me to stay* (he's the one who has asked me. Fr. C'est lui qui . . .).

It is perhaps worth while pointing out that the last syllable of an unstressed tail that would normally have a stress makes a slight but perceptible movement in the same direction as the preceding special stress. The word "stay" in the second example above echoes the stress on "He", dying away on a downward movement that may go below the normal lower range of the voice.

'HE wants me to stay.

This fact is of considerable importance for a natural reading of dialogue (see Exercises 141 to 145), and can be observed with increasing frequency throughout the rest of the exercises.

The teacher reads each sentence as marked, the student(s) reading it twice or three times after him:

1. *We* 'TRIED to make them listen
2. *I told* 'YOU to do it.
3. *I've drunk* 'YOUR coffee, I'm afraid.
4. *I* 'DON'T like porridge for-breakfast.
5. 'I told him not to come.
6. *They* 'ASKED me to come.
7. *Why don't you* 'BUY yourself a copy?
8. 'WE tried to make them listen.
9. 'I told you to do it.
10. *We're having* 'STRAWberries for tea today.
11. *I saw* 'MARGaret at the theatre last night.
12. *He brought me a* 'PRESent when he came home.
13. *He* 'RAN all the way to the station.
14. *The gardener has planted po*'TAtoes in the front garden.
15. *You've used to*'DAY'S newspaper to light the fire.
16. *There'll be* 'TEN guests to dinner tonight.
17. *They looked* 'EVerywhere for my wallet.
18. *He gave me a* 'NEW one instead of the old.
19. *He'll* 'NEVer do it any better.
20. *They are* 'FLYing to America.
21. *That's* 'NOT the best way to do it.
22. *He heard* 'YOU were here.
23. *They asked* 'ME to come.
24. *I* 'TOLD you who to write to.
25. *He re*'FUSED to bring the book back.

Exercise 68. Special Stress (Tune I, two stresses)

Note. See Exercises 65-67. If special emphasis is to be given to more than one point in a remark, the fall will be repeated. All the other syllables will remain unstressed. If one of these ideas carries more weight than the other, it will fall from a greater height. This will not be shown in the exercises; the teacher or student may read them as he wishes.

Pattern: `HE wants me to `STAY.   `HE wants `ME to stay.

> `HE wants me to `STAY (but SHE would like me to LEAVE).
>
> `HE wants `ME to stay (but SHE would like my FRIEND to).

The teacher reads each of these sentences with two special stresses as marked, the student(s) repeating it twice or three times after him:

1. `WE like `TEA.
2. `I'D like to try a`GAIN.
3. `HOLiday trains are `ALways crowded.
4. *He* `SAID he stayed late at the `OFFice.
5. *We had our* `LUNCH before we `GOT here.
6. *The* `LAST bus goes at `TEN o'clock.
7. `I prefer `COFFee.
8. `JOAN is engaged to `JOHN.
9. `NOW'S the time to `WORK.
10. `THIS book is `VERY interesting.
11. *He* `GENerally gets up at `SEVen o'clock.
12. *I'm afraid* `I shall have to `GO now.
13. *I* `THOUGHT she was `ILL.
14. `SOME children are afraid of the `DARK.
15. `SOME children are a`FRAID of the dark.

16. *I* `NEVer drink `WINE with my meals.
17. `I know a`NOTHer way.
18. *It's* `NOT so far as you `THINK.
19. *We* `MUSTn't forget to `TELL him about it.
20. *This* `ISn't the one I `WANTed.

Exercise 69. Special Stress (question-word questions)

Note. See Exercises 65-67. As with ordinary statements, the syllables up to the one with special stress may be spoken with normal stress and intonation, or they may be completely unstressed; the tail following the special stress is always unstressed. This exercise has the normal intonation (Tune I) as far as the special stress.

Pattern: ｜How many ｜people ｜came to `SEE you?

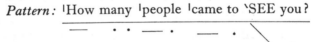

The teacher reads each question as marked, the student(s) repeating it twice or three times after him:

1. ｜Which is ｜your `COLDest month?
2. ｜Where have you ｜put my `GLASSes?
3. ｜Why do you ｜have to ｜leave at `ONCE?
4. ｜Which is the ｜platform for the `NINE o'clock train?
5. ｜Why ｜can't `YOU do it?
6. ｜How ｜much do `YOU think it costs?
7. ｜What's the ｜matter with `YOU?
8. ｜Who ｜told you to ｜wait `HERE?
9. ｜Which ｜kind is the `BEST?
10. ｜How ｜late will they `BE?
11. ｜What ｜date is `EASTer this year?
12. ｜Who is ｜going to `MEET them?
13. ｜Which would `YOU recommend?
14. ｜Where do you ｜keep the `COAL?

15. ˈWhy ˈdon't you ˋLISTen?
16. ˈHow ˈlong do you ˈwant to ˋKEEP it?
17. ˈWhen do the ˈchildren get ˋHOME?
18. ˈWhere are you ˈgoing on ˋSUNday?
19. ˈWhat's the ˈname of the ˋTALL girl?
20. ˈWhose ˈhouse are we ˈgoing to ˋTHIS time?

Exercise 70. Special Stress (question-word questions)

Note. See Exercise 69. As in the earlier examples of statements with a special stress, question-word questions can also be spoken entirely unstressed (except for the special stress itself) to give extra prominence to the point of the question.

Pattern: How many people came to ˋSEE *you?*

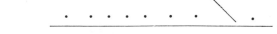

The variants shown in the note to Exercise 64 also apply to question-word questions.

The teacher reads each question as marked, the student(s) repeating it twice or three times after him:

1. *Which is your* ˋCOLDest month?
2. *Why can't* ˋYOU do it?
3. *When is* ˋPETer's birthday?
4. *Who* ˋTOLD you to wait here?
5. *What* ˋFOR?
6. *What have* ˋI got to do with it?
7. *What's* ˋTHAT for?
8. *Who came in* ˋFIRST in that race?
9. *Why do you* ˋHAVE to go at once?
10. *Which is the platform for the* ˋNINE o'clock train?
11. *How much do* ˋYOU think it costs?
12. *Where have* ˋYOU been?

13. *What's the* `MATTer *with you?*
14. *How* `LATE *will they be?*
15. *Why should* `YOU *bother?*
16. *Why* `NOT?
17. *What was* `WRONG *with it?*
18. *Which would* `YOU *recommend?*
19. *Where do you keep the* `COAL?
20. *Where are* `YOU *going on Sunday?*
21. *Why don't you* `LISTen?
22. *Why* `SHOULD I?
23. *When do the* `CHILDren *get home?*
24. *Whose house are we going to* `THIS *time?*
25. *Why do we always go* `THERE?

Exercise 71. Special Stress (question-word questions)

Note: See Exercises 69 and 70. The pattern of Exercise 70 is here set down with two special stresses; the rest of the sentence is unstressed.

Pattern: What have `YOU *got to do with* `HIS *problems?*

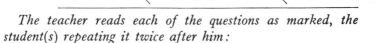

The teacher reads each of the questions as marked, the student(s) repeating it twice after him:

1. `WHY *must you go* `NOW?
2. `WHERE *did you put* `MY *hat?*
3. *What will* `MOTHer *say when* `SHE *hears?*
4. *What* `WILL *mother say when she* `HEARS?
5. *When* `ARE *you going to stop that* `NOISE?
6. *Who would have* `THOUGHT *it could be* done so `QUICKly?
7. *Which* `DRESS *shall I put on for the* `PARty?
8. *Why* `CAN'T *she be more* `REAsonable?
9. *How am* `I *to know what* `HE *means?*

10. *Where's the* `RED book I left on the `TAble?
11. `WHERE ought `HE to sit?
12. `WHO forgot to wipe their `SHOES?
13. `WHY didn't she re`FUSE to tell them?
14. *How* `DOES she manage to keep so `SLIM?
15. *When did your* `YOUNGest daughter be`GIN to learn the piano?

Exercise 72. Personal Element (in question-word questions)

Note. We have already noted the general difference between Tunes I and II.

I. Definite factual assertion; objectivity.

II. The addition of some personal element (doubt, query, reproach, concession, innuendoes of all kinds); lack of finality. Question-word questions are mainly of an objective character in that they do not ask for or offer an opinion (which is personal) but a fact. But questions made by verb-inversion (do you? can he? etc.) demand "yes" or "no" for an answer, and by seeking an opinion are therefore personal in character. So for the former we normally use Tune I (Exercise 49 and others), and for the latter the normal pattern is with Tune II (Exercises 53-57 and others).

Pattern: We frequently use Tune II for question-word questions if our mental attitude to the question causes some personal element to be prominent. For example, the question:

ᴵWhat is your `**name**?

is here in its normal pattern asking for information of a factual nature, such as an official filling up a form.

ᴵWhat is your ˏ**name**?

is a form showing some interest or sympathy, and might be so used to invite the confidence of a lost child. It is a very usual intonation when question-word questions are used in the little exchanges of everyday conversation, expressing and inviting extra warmth and interest.

The teacher reads each of the following question-word questions using Tune II as shown, the student(s) repeating it twice or three times after him:

ˈwhere do you ˌlive? / ˈwhat did you ˌsay? / ˈhow ˌold are you? / ˈwhen have you ˌtime? / ˈwhat can I ˌdo for you? / ˈwhat's the ˌmatter? / ˈwhy do you ˌwant to? / ˈwhich ˈcoat is ˌyours? / ˈwhy ˈdon't you ˌknow? / ˈhow did you ˈmanage to ˈbe so ˌlate? / ˈwhen do you ˈget ˌup? / ˈwhat ˈtime shall I ˌcome? / ˈwhere shall we ˌmeet? / ˈwhy ˈwasn't it ˌfinished? / ˈwhich ˈcake would you ˌlike? / ˈwhat have you ˈgot ˌthere? / ˈhow ˈmuch do they ˌcharge? / ˈwhen ˈmay I ˌgo? / ˈwhere am ˈI to ˌsit? / ˈwho should I ˌwrite to? / ˈwhen can I ˌphone you? / ˈwhat's your ˌnumber? / ˈwhat's ˈgot to be ˈdone ˌnext? / ˈwho do you ˈwant to ˈsee ˌnow? / ˈwhere were ˈyou ˌlast year? / ˈhow ˈmuch does ˌthis cost? / ˈwhen's the ˈbest ˈtime to ˌcome? / ˈwhat would you ˈlike to ˌdrink? / ˈwho'd ˈlike aˌnother one?

Exercise 73. Personal Element (question-word questions)

Note. Another important use of Tune II for question-word questions is that used in a question that is asked for the **second time**. The question-word itself begins on the low tone, lending emphasis to the whole question. The question has been repeated either because the answer has sounded improbable, or because the speaker has forgotten the answer. All the syllables except the first are virtually unstressed, and will be written so in the exercises; but as always in sentences with long "tails", trace of the former stress and rhythm can still be felt, as suggested in the pattern below:

Pattern: ,**What** is your name? ╱ ‾‾‾‾ · · · or ╱ · · ╱

The teacher reads each of the sentences in Exercise 72 as shown in the first few examples below, the student(s) repeating it twice or three times after him:

,**where** do you live? | ,**what** did you say? | ,**how** old are you? | ,**when** have you time? | *etc. taking examples from the previous exercise.*

Exercise 74. Personal Element (question-word questions)

Note: See previous two exercises.

Patterns for question-word questions.

Normal: ˈWhat is your ˋ**name**?

Interested: ˈWhat is your ,**name**?

Repeated: ,**What** is your name?

Repeat Exercise 72 in the normal intonation of question-word questions, as in the first few examples below:

ˈwhere do you ˋ**live**? | ˈwhat did you ˋ**say**? | ˈhow ˋ**old** are you? | ˈwhen have you ˋ**time**? | ˈwhat can I ˋ**do** for you? | *etc. etc. taking examples from Exercise 72.*

Exercise 75. Personal Element (inversion questions)

Note. Questions made by inverting verb and subject (yes-no questions) are normally spoken on Tune II (see Exercises 53-57 and others). By their nature they are partly personal because they invite the other person's opinion ("yes" or "no"), and in a sense they are incomplete because the complementary question ("or not?" etc.) is implied. Nevertheless we often hear such questions spoken with Tune I. The two principal situations where this intonation is heard with yes-no questions are:

1. **Rhetorical questions** (expecting agreement and not asking an opinion).

2. **Assertive remarks**, almost commands; often to keep someone to the point.

Patterns for these types:

1. ˈAren't they ˋ**pre**tty? (They obviously are!)

2a. ˈHave you ˈbrought my ˋ**coat**?　(I asked you for it; I expect it.)

2b. *Yes, but* ˈwill he ˋ**come**?

A. " *He's* ˈvery ˋ**charm**ing; *I'm* ˈsure you'll ˋ**like** him."

B. " *Yes, but* ˈwill he ˋ**come**? " (Never mind the description; come to the point that interests me!)

The teacher reads each of the following inversion questions with Tune I as shown, the student(s) repeating it twice or three times after him:

1. ˈIsn't that ˋ**kind** of her?
2. ˈWon't they be ˋ**pleased**?
3. ˈHaven't I been ˋ**quick**?
4. ˈDid you ˈdo as I ˋ**said**?
5. ˈWasn't it a ˈgood ˋ**film**?
6. ˈDon't they look ˋ**nice**?

7. ˈIsn't it a ˎpity?
8. ˈDoes it ˎmatter?
9. ˈWasn't the ˈweather ˎawful?
10. ˈWeren't we ˈwell ˎlooked after?
11. ˈDo you aˎgree?
12. ˈAren't I ˎnaughty?¹
13. *But* ˈare you ˎsure?
14. ˈCan it be ˎhelped?
15. ˈWould it be a ˎgood thing to do?
16. ˈWon't it be ˎwonderful?
17. ˈIsn't it ˎlovely today?
18. ˈWasn't that a ˎdifficult examination?
19. ˈAren't you ˎsmart this evening?
20. ˈDid you ˈput the ˎkettle on?
21. ˈCan you ˈdo it by your ˎself?
22. ˈDoes she ˈknow the ˎway?
23. ˈAm I ˎlate?
24. ˈMay I ˈask a ˎquestion?
25. ˈDo you ˈthink that's ˎright?

Exercise 76. **Personal Element** (inversion questions)

Note. See Exercise 75. An emphatic form of these inversion questions with Tune I has its big downward leap on the verbal inversion (usually the first word). The rest of the sentence remains low and is unstressed, although the original rhythm is still quietly felt.

Pattern: ˎAREN'T they pretty?   *Yes but* ˎWILL he come?

The teacher reads each of the following questions in the given stressed form, the student(s) repeating it twice or three times after him:

¹ Seldom said by men. Usually a playful apology.

'ISN'T that kind of her? / 'WON'T they be pleased? / 'HAVEN'T I been quick? / 'DON'T they look nice? / 'ISn't it a pity? / 'AREN'T I naughty? / *but* 'ARE you sure? / 'WOULD it be a good thing to do? / 'WON'T it be wonderful? / 'ISn't it lovely today? / 'DOES she know the way?

Exercise 77. Special Stress (Tune II, inversion questions)

Note. A common use of this is the emphatic form of questions spoken with Tune II. The most usual pattern has the emphatic leap down on the inverted verb (normally the first word), the rest of the sentence rising on a series of unstressed syllables. The last syllable that would normally have been stressed retains a shadow of its former importance, and for this reason will still be marked as stressed. It is felt and heard not so much as a heavier accent but rather as a more definite lift in the rising intonation. The key patterns will make this clearer. This emphatic question pattern with Tune II is used mainly for questions repeated (either for insistence on an answer or because the original answer has been forgotten or wasn't clear); or in order to ask the question in a very doubtful manner.

Patterns: 1. 'HAVE you seen my ⸝hat?

'HAVE you seen my ⸝hat? (Please think! I'm sure you must have.)

N.B.—The final rise will be shown by the usual accent, but the word taking it will be printed in italics to indicate that it is almost without stress, though spoken with a well-defined rise.

An alternative pattern is:

'HAVE you seen my ⸝hat?

2. `DID she say ‚six o'clock?

`DID she say ‚six o'clock? (I'm not quite sure what she said.)

The teacher reads each of the following questions of Tune II type with special emphasis on the verbal inversion, the student(s) repeating it twice or three times after him:

`IS it the ‚fourteenth today? / `CAN you do it by your-‚self? / `DOES she know the ‚way? / `WOULD it be a ‚good thing to do? / `WOULD it be a good thing to ‚do? / `DO you think that's ‚right? / `MAY I ask a ‚question? / `WOULD you have preferred the ‚green one? / `SHOULD I have informed the ‚police? / `ARE they going a‚way? / `WILL it be too late to buy ‚tickets? / `DID you turn the ‚light out? / `DID you put the ‚kettle on? / `WERE you ‚really ill? / `IS it the house we went to be‚fore? / `WAS it the house I ‚told you about? / `IS smoking pro‚hibited here? / `WAS I right, after ‚all? / `COULD you come again ‚next week?

Exercise 78. Special Stress (Tune II, question-word questions)

Note. See Exercises 77 and 73. The pattern practised in Exercise 73 is given added emphasis by using the intonation of Exercise 77, the special emphasis being given to the question-word. The syllable that would normally have been the last stressed one again takes added lift, and will be shown in print in italics preceded by the Tune II rising stress-mark.

Pattern: `WHAT is your ‚name?   `WHAT is your ‚name?

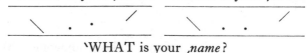

`WHAT is your ‚name?

The teacher reads each of the following questions, taken from Exercise 73, with special emphasis on the question-word, the student(s) repeating it twice or three times after him:

'WHERE do you ‚live? / 'WHAT did you ‚say? / 'WHAT can I ‚do for you? / 'WHAT'S the ‚matter? / 'WHY do you ‚want to? / 'HOW did you manage to be so ‚late? / 'WHERE shall we ‚meet? / 'WHAT have you got ‚there? / 'HOW much do they ‚charge? / 'WHEN may I ‚go? / 'WHERE am I to ‚sit? / 'WHO should I ‚write to? / 'WHAT'S your ‚phone number? / 'WHO do you want to see ‚next? / 'WHAT would you like to ‚drink?

Exercise 79. Special Stress (emphatic questions compared)

Note. From the earlier exercises on questions we can see that question-word questions are normally spoken with Tune I, and inversion (yes-no) questions with Tune II. For special reasons, however, these patterns can be reversed (see Exercises 72, 73 and 75). The patterns of Exercises 73 and 75 occur with both types of question as follows:

Patterns: A. ‚**Do** you know the answer?

"Yes-no" question showing great doubt or uncertainty; or asked for the second time.

B. 'DO you know the answer?

Insistent form, to keep someone to the point.

A. ‚**Where** do you want to go?

Question-word question in its repeated form (Ex. 73).

B. ‘WHERE do you want to go?

Insistent form, to keep someone to the point.

The teacher reads each of the following questions on the rising pattern A above, the student(s) repeating it twice after him:

1. ‚**Have** you got enough time?
2. ‚**Was** she really ill?
3. ‚**Will** anyone want to go?
4. ‚**Have** you locked the front door?
5. ‚**Are** we to expect any more money?
6. ‚**Have** you enough knives and forks?
7. ‚**What** are you going to tell him?
8. ‚**Where** can we put them?
9. ‚**Who's** going to carry them?
10. ‚**When** will the house be finished?
11. ‚**Would** they agree to such a plan?
12. ‚**Do** people believe he was responsible?
13. ‚**Which** book is the most suitable?
14. ‚**Why** does he refuse to listen?
15. ‚**Could** it be done any other way?
16. ‚**Was** it wise to leave her all alone?
17. ‚**Is** there any difference between them?
18. ‚**Did** he tell you the result?
19. ‚**Who** is going to support him?
20. ‚**Is** there any reason why we should?
21. ‚**Who** do you think was to blame?

22. ‚**Where** were we supposed to put the cases?
23. ‚**Who** told you to wait for an answer?
24. ‚**Was** there any chance of succeeding?
25. ‚**Had** they done all they could?

Exercise 80. Special Stress (emphatic questions compared)

Note. See previous exercise and Exercise 76.

Pattern: The emphatic falling pattern B of the notes to the previous exercise is heard when the speaker insists on getting an immediate answer, probably after a digression from the point. The situation can easily be implied by introducing the question with an unstressed " *Yes, but. . .*"

Yes, but ʻDO you know the answer?

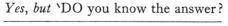

The teacher reads each of the questions in Exercise 79 in the above pattern, introducing it with " Yes, but. . . ." The student(s) will repeat it twice after him. The first half-dozen sentences are shown below:

1. *Yes, but* ʻHAVE you got enough time?
2. *Yes, but* ʻWAS she really ill?
3. *Yes, but* ʻWILL anyone want to go?
4. *Yes, but* ʻHAVE you locked the front door?
5. *Yes, but* ʻARE we to expect any more money?
6. *Yes, but* ʻHAVE you enough knives and forks?

· . . . *and similarly with the rest of Exercise* 79.

Exercise 81. Special Stress (implications)

Note. See Exercises 65 and 67 for comments on the weakened rhythm of the unstressed portion of sentences with a special stress. This point is of some importance for the proper understanding of special stress with Tune II.

Patterns: I ˈknew he ˈwasn't ˈpresent.

(Objective statement with Tune I).

I ˈKNEW he wasn't present.

(Special stress to make the speaker's certainty prominent.)

N.B.—Although "he wasn't present" is now shown as un-stressed, the original stressing of ". . . . he ˈwasn't ˈpresent" is still weakly perceptible. If the speaker wishes to give some personal feeling to the statement in the form of an unspoken hint or innuendo, he will use Tune II, the rise occurring **on what would normally have been the last significant stress.** So the example would become:

I ˈKNEW he wasn't ˌpresent.

(. . . . although people have tried to persuade me that he was.)

The stress on "present" is not strong but the rise of Tune II beginning on that word is quite definite and unmistakable. The final can rise can also take place over the last syllable itself . . .

I ˈKNEW he wasn't ˌthere.

. . . . or the rise can also occur over several syllables.

I think 'TEA'S the ‚**best** thing to drink.

(I hope you agree with me!)

In some form or another the emphatic pattern of Tune II is extremely common in English, as we so often make remarks which carry with them some implication which is not put into words but is quite clearly expressed by the final rising intonation. The next few exercises will offer systematic practice material on the principal varieties of Special Stress with **Tune II**.

The first group has its special stress on the first syllable and a rise on the last syllable.

The teacher reads each statement as indicated, the student(s) repeating it twice or three times after him:

'THAT'S not the one I ‚**want** / 'MY way is the ‚**best** / 'WE are to blame for ‚**that** / 'SOMEone must know the ‚**truth** / 'PETer is the man to ‚**ask** / 'THAT wasn't what she ‚**meant** / 'YOU ought to ‚**know** / 'THAT'S not the way to fry an ‚**egg** / 'I have nothing to ‚**say** / 'NOW is the time to ‚**act** / 'SOON we shall know where we ‚**are** / 'FARMers will like this ‚**rain** / 'NObody'll notice ‚**that** / 'SKI-ing's the sport for ‚**you** / 'THERE'S the ‚**sea** / 'HERE'S my little ‚**boy!** / 'THIS is my ‚**son** / 'THERE'S St. **Paul's!** / 'ALL children have to do as they're ‚**told** / 'THIS material's very ‚**poor** / 'TOM will want to ‚**know** / 'ASpirin will do you ‚**good** / 'MAYbe I could ‚**come** / 'NORMally I ‚**can** / 'YOU won't be there to ‚**see** / 'THIS hat isn't ‚**bad** / 'THURSday would be a good ‚**day** / 'THAT'S not the ‚**way** / 'BLUE'S a good colour for a ‚**blonde** / 'MEAT'S getting very ‚**dear.**

Exercise 82. Special Stress (implications)

Note. See previous exercise.

Pattern: the final rise spread over two or more syllables.

ʻTHAT might be ˏ**poss**ible.   ʻHERE'S the one you ˏ**want**ed.

The teacher reads each statement as indicated, the student(s) repeating it two or three times after him:

ʻTHAT'S a good sugˏ**gest**ion / ʻHERE'S the book I'm ˏ**study**ing / ʻMY tea is ˏ**sweet** enough / ʻTHAT'S not the way to ˏ**do** it / ʻWE were the first to reˏ**mind** him of it / ʻKNITting is quite a ˏ**pleas**ant occupation / ʻHE'LL never underˏ**stand** them / ʻTHIS is the way to ˏ**do** it / ʻHERE'S a nice place for a ˏ**pic**nic / ʻNObody could have done ˏ**better** / ʻNOW'S the ˏ**mo**ment / ʻYOURS ought to come toˏ**mor**row / ʻYESterday you said you'd ˏ**let** me / ʻWE don't think it'll be ˏ**poss**ible / ʻYOU'LL have to pay for the ˏ**dam**age / ʻTHIS book is very ˏ**inter**esting / ʻHE ought to be able to reˏ**mem**ber / ʻSPRING is very lovely in **Eng**land / ʻMOST people prefer riding to ˏ**walk**ing / ʻHERE'S your ˏ**mack**intosh / ʻSOME of us aˏ**greed** to it / ʻNO-one listens to ˏ**moth**er / ʻMY house is the ˏ**near**est / ʻTHERE'S the Tower of ˏ**Lond**on! / ʻSOMEbody must know who ˏ**did** it / ʻWE have nothing aˏ**gainst** it / ʻMANY students find this exercise pretty ˏ**diff**icult / ʻTHIS is my ˏ**daugh**ter / ʻGAS stoves are more ecoˏ**nom**ical.

Exercise 83. Special Stress (implications)

Note. See Exercise 81.

Pattern: the special stress not on the first syllable.

He doesn't ʻWANT to see you ˏ**now**.   ... see you ˏ**next** week.

The teacher reads each sentence as indicated, the student(s) repeating it two or three times after him:

You `CAN if you ,**want** to / *you* `CAN if you ,**like** / *these* po`TAtoes are very ,**dear** / *holidays a*`BROAD are more ex,**cit**ing / *holidays a*`BROAD are more ,**fun** / *it would be* `LOVEly to have a flat of one's ,**own** / *I'm afraid* `HE won't be able to ,**help** you / *I doubt if* `THAT'S any ,**good** / *it's not* `POSSible to work any ,**harder** / *it's not* `POSSible to work any ,**more** / *you* `CAN'T sing songs on a ,**bus** / *you* `CAN'T sing songs during ,**dinn**er / *I don't think it's* `RIGHT to re,**fuse** / *it was only* `YESterday they decided ,**not** to / *it's* `DOUBTful whether she'll suc,**ceed** / *I was* `MOST surprised to ,**hear** it / *he usually* `ASKS if he ,**wants** anything / *we didn't* `KNOW it would be so ,**diff**icult / *we didn't* `KNOW it would be so ,**hard** / *you* `MUST try to be more ,**care**ful / *it's the* `GRAMophone that needs re,**pair**ing / *but you* `TOLD me it was time to ,**go** / *I didn't* `KNOW it had to be written in ,**ink** / *we never* `THOUGHT of buying a ,**car** / *the food at the* `OTHer hotel was ,**bett**er.

Exercise 84. Special Stress (implications)

Note. See Exercises 81-83. The final rise of the last three exercises is very often given special prominence, too. In this exercise this second special stress extends over two or more syllables.

Patterns: *That's* `NOT the piece I `WANTed you to ,**play**.

That's `NOT the piece I `WANTed you to ,**play**
. . . (but I enjoyed it nevertheless).

I 'CAN'T come on 'TUES,**day**

I 'CAN'T come on 'TUES,**day** . . . (perhaps another day will do).

It is clear from this last example that the final rise can occur on an unstressed syllable; as this, however, is the syllable that gives this intonation pattern its special quality that we have loosely called an implication, it will continue to appear in bold type throughout the exercises.

The teacher reads each sentence as indicated, the student(s) repeating it two or three times after him:

this radio is 'MUCH better than the 'OTHer one you ,**had** | *mother* 'NEVer allowed me to put my 'ELbows on the ,**table** | *we* 'CAN'T afford to 'GIVE them a,**way** | *it wouldn't be* po'LITE to 'TELephone ,**him** | *it* 'WOULD be fun to have a 'BIRTHday ,**par**ty | *I* 'DON'T go to work on 'SUN,**day** | *I* 'NEVer take sugar in 'CO,**coa** | *I* 'ALways take sugar in 'COF,**fee** | *he* 'PROMised to be 'PUNC,**tual** | *it* 'LOOKED like rain this 'MORN,**ing** | *he* 'NEVer drinks whisky for 'BREAK,**fast** | *we* 'THOUGHT you would all be 'UP by six o',**clock** | *I* 'OUGHT to go to the 'DENTist's ,**soon** | *I* 'CAN'T work 'EVery minute of the ,**day** | *one* ex'PECTS the weather to be bad in 'JAN,**uary** | *we can't* af'FORD to buy a 'NEW ,**one** | *I* 'KNEW it would be 'DIFFi,**cult** | *we'll have a* 'SPECial cake on my 'BIRTH,**day** | *you* 'SUREly don't practise for 'THREE hours every ,**day** | *I didn't* 'MEAN to eat 'ALL the apple-,**pie** | *she* 'NEVer goes out with her 'HUS,**band** | 'THAT'S why they wouldn't 'LISTen ,**to** me.

Exercise 85. Special Stress (implications)

Note. See Exercise 84. Very often the second "special stress" of
this type of sentence falls on the same syllable as the rising
intonation. This produces what is sometimes called a **wave
intonation**, and can be most easily practised over long open
syllables such as this exercise consists of.

Pattern: She `NEVer drinks ᵛTEA. . .   (so it's useless to
                                                   offer her any)

(the voice makes the fall for the stress on "tea", and
immediately afterwards makes the rise for Tune II on the
same syllable. Note the sign ᵛ to show a syllable with this
fall-rise or wave intonation in print).

The implications suggested by a speaker using Tune II in one
of its stressed forms are of all possible kinds. In this exercise
the unspoken thought implied by the final rise (of the wave) is
added in small type to each sentence.

*The teacher reads each sentence as shown, the student(s)
repeating it twice or three times after him. A suggested
implication follows in small type; it is there merely to help
the reader to put the remark in a natural context, and should
not be read aloud:*

1. *Well, I* `DON'T aᵛGREE
        (though I do understand your point of view)
2. *You* `OUGHT to ᵛTRY
        (even if you're not likely to succeed)
3. *You* `ARE ᵛSLOW
        (I should have thought you would have been quicker)
4. *It'd be* `BETTer to ᵛFLY.
        (although the journey is very beautiful by train)
5. *You* `NEEDn't ᵛPAY
        (so don't be put off by the thought of the expense)

6. *I* `ONLY had ͮTHREE
  (and you knew that wasn't enough)
7. *I* `LOVE `KNITT͵ing, | *but I* `CAN'T ͮSEW
8. *I'd* `LOVE to ͮGO
  (if only it were possible)
9. *He's* `NEVer ͮSURE
  (so it wouldn't be wise to rely on him)
10. *It's* `MUCH too ͮHIGH
  (we like the hill, but we aren't likely to get to the top)
11. *I* `DON'T believe it's ͮTRUE
  (in spite of all the rumours)
12. *She* `CAN'T come toͮDAY
  (it's a pity; what about another day?)
13. *It* `DOESn't look ͮNEW
  (but it seems all right, though)
14. *That question's* `TOO hard for ͮME
  (but no doubt someone else can manage it)
15. *It would be* `NICE if you could ͮSTAY
  (but I suppose you really must go)
16. *I'm afraid that's* `ALL we can ͮDO
  (I'm sorry it's not very much)
17. *I* `DIDn't think she was ͮSHY
  (whatever else she might be)
18. *I'd* `LIKE to come if I ͮMAY
  (I hope there's no objection)
19. *She has* `PRETTy ͮHAIR
  (though I don't admire much else about her)
20. *I'd* `LIKE it if it's ͮBLUE
  (but I'm not interested in having any other colour)

Exercise 86. Special Stress (implications)

Note. See Exercises 84 and 85. Here is the same pattern with the "wave" over long closed syllables. This time the implications will be left to the speaker's imagination.

Pattern: I `DON'T want to be ˅LATE:

I `DON'T want to be ˅LATE (. . . . so **please** excuse my hurrying away so soon)

The teacher reads each sentence as shown, the student(s) repeating it twice or three times after him.

1. *I'm sur*`PRISED she didn't leave a ˅NOTE.
2. *She'd have* `COME if she'd ˅KNOWN.
3. *I've* `NOT come to ˅TALK.
4. *I couldn't* `POSSibly eat any ˅MORE.
5. *You'd* `BETTer turn off the ˅LIGHT.
6. *I* `HOPE you're not ˅BORED.
7. *I* `KNEW you were a˅LONE.
8. *That's* `NOT quite the ˅SAME.
9. *He re*`FUSED to go by ˅PLANE.
10. `MINE are smaller than ˅YOURS.
11. *Yours are* `LARGer than ˅MINE.
12. *You didn't* `SAY you had to ˅LEAVE.
13. *It* `MUST be finished in ˅TIME.
14. *He* `ALways sings out of ˅TUNE.
15. *They're al*`READY out of ˅SIGHT.
16. *I can't* `THINK what I've done with ˅MINE.
17. *This bread seems* `VERy ˅STALE.
18. *She looks* `VERy ˅TIRED.
19. *We're* `NOT going out in the ˅RAIN.
20. *You* `NEEDn't wait in the ˅STREET.
21. *I'd* `RATHer go by ˅TRAIN.
22. *I ex*`PECT he'll be ˅LATE.
23. *I* `DON'T think you're ˅RIGHT.
24. *I don't know* `WHAT to ˅CHOOSE.
25. *Well, I* `DON'T suppose she ˅CARES.

Exercise 87. Special Stress (implications)

Note. See Exercises 84-86. Here is the same pattern with the "wave" over a final short syllable.

Pattern: Well, I `DON'T like the look of ᵛTHAT.

Well, I `DON'T like the look of ᵛTHAT (an understatement for "I think the situation looks bad").

The teacher reads each sentence as shown, the student(s) repeating it twice or three times after him:

1. *We* `CAN'T ask ᵛTHEM.
2. *I* `WOULD if I ᵛCOULD.
3. *We* `KNOW where it ᵛIS.
4. *I* `SHOULDn't do it like ᵛTHAT.
5. *You're* `MUCH fatter than ᵛJOHN.
6. *I want to* `FINish it if I ᵛCAN.
7. *I'm afraid there's* `NOwhere to ᵛSIT.
8. *I* `DON'T expect she ᵛWILL.
9. *I* `DON'T think they ᵛHAVE.
10. *I* `DIDN'T think she ᵛWOULD.
11. *I* `WILL if I ᵛCAN.
12. *I* `KNEW he was ᵛILL.
13. *I should* `LIKE a little more ᵛHAM.
14. *There's* `NOT enough left for the ᵛCAT.
15. *I* `CAN'T lend you a ᵛPEN.
16. *I* `ONLy speak French when I ᵛMUST.
17. *You've given me* `RATHer a ᵛLOT.
18. *You didn't* `TELL me what he ᵛDID.
19. `NObody knew what it ᵛWAS.
20. *We never* `THOUGHT he'd live so ᵛLONG.
21. *He's* `ALways willing to lend a ᵛHAND.
22. *Your dog looks* `VERy well ᵛFED.

23. *I* 'WONder if I ⌄SHALL.
24. *I* 'KNOW he's very well ⌄READ.
25. *I* 'DIDN'T think he ⌄WOULD.
26. *I* 'COULDn't keep your dinner very ⌄HOT.
27. *You* 'CAN'T keep it in a ⌄JUG.
28. *You'll miss the* 'BUS if you don't ⌄RUN.
29. *They hadn't* i'MAGined it would be so ⌄BIG.
30. *I* 'DOUBT if she ever ⌄WILL.
31. *I* 'HOPE you won't get ⌄WET.
32. *You must* 'GIVE him one that ⌄FITS.
33. *You* 'CAN'T go without a ⌄HAT.
34. *I* 'HOPE you can ⌄COME.
35. *It's the* 'OTHer sister that works in a ⌄SHOP.

Exercise 88. Special Stress (implications)

Note. The last 6 exercises practise the most usual stressed forms of Tune II, finishing with those patterns where the special stress falls on the same syllable that takes the rising intonation; these two factors together produce the characteristic "wave" intonation—a combined fall and rise on one syllable. This exercise contains all the types we have practised.

Patterns:

I 'HOPE you won't ,**mind**.

I 'HOPE you won't ,**lose** it.

I 'HOPE you won't ⌄**MIND**.

It's 'NOT so far as I 'THOUGHT it would have ,**been**.

It's 'NOT so far as I ᵛTHOUGHT.

The teacher reads each of the following sentences with the given intonation, the student(s) repeating it twice or three times after him:

1. *I* 'WILL if you ᵛLIKE.
2. *I* 'WILL if you 'WANT me ,**to**.
3. 'THAT'S how it stands as far as we can ᵛTELL.
4. 'THAT'S how it stands as far as 'WE can ,**tell**.
5. 'THAT'S not the way 'I ,**look** at it.
6. *You* 'TOLD me not to 'TELL ,**anyone**.
7. 'I wouldn't do it if 'I were ,**you**.
8. *There's no knowing* 'WHAT he'll be up to ᵛNEXT.
9. *I* 'DO hope it's all ,**right**.
10. *I* 'DO hope you can ᵛSTAY.
11. *I sup*'POSE I ,**must**.
12. *You* 'MIGHT have said so beᵛFORE.
13. *It's* 'MUCH harder than I ex'PECT,**ed**.
14. *They're not* 'USually so ,**late**.
15. *He said the goods were* 'SURE to arrive toᵛDAY.
16. *I meant to have* 'FINished it this after,**noon**.
17. *I* 'HOPE you won't do it aᵛGAIN.
18. *It's just as well she* 'WASn't working 'LATE to,**night**.
19. *I* 'THOUGHT I should be in ,**time**.
20. 'NObody knows what he 'MEANT ,**by** it.
21. *They're* 'SURE to have left 'SOMEthing be,**hind**.
22. *It's* 'ALL very well to make 'PROMis,**es**.
23. *We* 'ALL hope you'll ᵛCOME.

24. *I* 'SHOULDn't be too ‿SURE. (*I* 'SHOULDn't be ‿'TOO ‚**sure**.)
25. *He'll* 'NEVer agree to ‿THAT.
26. *I don't know* 'WHAT 'MOTHer will ‚**say**.
27. *It's not* 'FAIR to expect me to do 'ALL the ‚**work**.
28. *I'd never have be*'LIEVED you could have been so ‚**self**ish.
29. *One's* 'NEVer too old to 'LEARN, you ‚**know**.
30. *It's not* 'QUITE the ‚**same**.
31. *He* 'USED to live ‚**here**.
32. *She might have* 'KNOWN it would be ‚**use**less.
33. *I'm* 'SURE you're ‿WRONG.
34. *It isn't* 'FAIR to keep it all your‚**self**.
35. 'YOU ought to ‚**know**.
36. *It's not the way* 'WE ‚**look** at it.
37. *I'd never have* 'GUESSED it was ‿HER.
38. *I'll* 'TRY to be ‚**care**ful.
39. *He* 'HAD to ‿TRY.
40. *That's* 'ALL very ‿WELL, | *but . . .*
    It 'MAY be ‿TRUE, | *but . . .*
41. *It's* 'NO use 'GRUMB‚**ling**.
42. *That's the* 'SECond time you've trodden on my ‚**toe**.
43. *There's something be*'HIND all ‚**this**.
44. *I'm not* 'SURE that I ‚**can**. *I'm* 'NOT sure that I ‿CAN.
45. *He* 'WON'T believe what 'YOU ‚**say**.
46. *You* 'KNOW my opinion of ‿HER.
47. *I* 'SHOULDn't give it to 'HIM if I were ‚**you**.
48. *I* 'SHOULDn't give it to ‿HIM.
49. *I* 'HOPE you haven't for'GOTten ‚**me**.
50. *You* 'SAID be‿FORE | *that you* ‿WOULD.

Exercise 89. Imperatives

Note. An imperative, being a definite command, is normally spoken with Tune I.

ᅵShut the ˋ**door**! ᅵDon't ᅵgo aˋ**way**! ᅵLet's ᅵgo ˋ**home**!

In order not sound abrupt or rude, we use various combinations of intonation and grammatical devices that soften the command and change it into a kind of request. The principal devices are set out for practice in the following six exercises.

Pattern: The imperative can be turned into a request by using Tune II.

ᅵShut the ˏ**door**!   ᅵDon't ᅵgo a ˏ**way**!   .ᅵTake a ˏ**noth**er one!

Read each of the following commands twice in the same manner.

ᅵBring me a ˏ**chair**! / ᅵhurry ˏ**up**! / ᅵsing us a ˏ**song**! / ᅵdon't ˏ**cry**! / ᅵnever ˏ**mind**! / ᅵget on with your ˏ**dinn**er! / ᅵhold ˏ**this** for me! / ᅵdon't be ˏ**late**! / ᅵsit ˏ**down**! / ᅵhelp your ˏ**self**! / ᅵhave a ˏ**try**! / *now* ᅵlisten ˏ**care**fully! / ᅵget ˏ**up**! / ᅵwork ˏ**hard**! / ᅵgive me a ˏ**hand**! / ᅵwait a ˏ**mom**ent! / ᅵbuy me a ˏ**news**paper! / ᅵdon't be ˏ**silly**! / ᅵcome a ˏ**long**! / ᅵdon't be ˏ**lazy**! / ᅵlet's ᅵtry a ˏ**gain**! / ᅵmind the ˏ**step**! / ᅵstay where you ˏ**are**! / ᅵeat ˏ**up**! / ᅵopen the ˏ**wind**ow! / ᅵlend me your ˏ**pen**knife! / ᅵsee if you ˏ**can**! / ᅵdon't ˏ**look**! / ᅵbring it ˏ**here**! / ᅵtake ˏ**care**! / ᅵlight the ˏ**fire**! / ᅵmind what you're ˏ**do**ing! / ᅵturn on the ˏ**wire**less! / ᅵbe a ˏ**sport**! / ᅵhave a ˏ**heart**! / ᅵdon't be a ˏ**fraid**!

Exercise 90. Imperatives

Note. The question-tags "will you?" or "won't you?" are frequently combined with commands to soften them.

Pattern: Negative command (Tune II): "Will you?" (Tune I.)

ᴵDon't go a‚way, | ‵will you?

Read each of the following twice or three times after the above pattern. The tag "will you?" on a falling intonation is to be used throughout—it is only printed in the first example:

'Don't 'start ‚yet | ‵will you? / 'don't 'make a ‚noise . . . / 'don't stay up 'too ‚late . . . / 'don't for‚get . . . / 'don't ‚worry . . . / 'don't ‚hurry . . . / 'don't 'throw it a‚way . . . / 'don't 'listen to ‚her . . . / 'don't 'eat any ‚more . . . / 'don't 'spend it ‚all . . . / 'don't ‚break it . . . / 'don't 'take any ‚notice . . . / 'don't 'cut it any ‚shorter . . . / 'don't go 'out in the ‚rain . . . / 'don't 'wait for ‚me . . . / 'don't ‚waste it . . . / 'don't be ‚long . . . / 'don't 'let him ‚go . . . / 'don't ‚drop it . . . / 'don't be up‚set . . . / 'don't 'wander off the ‚path . . . / 'don't 'lift it if it's 'too ‚heavy . . . / 'don't 'tease your 'little ‚brother . . . / 'don't dis'turb the ‚baby . . .

Exercise 91. Imperatives

Pattern: The negative commands of Exercise 90 can be given a strong feeling of personal entreaty by using the stressed form of Tune II (introduced at Exercise 81).

‵DON'T go a‚way | ‵will you?

Read Exercise 90 *again, making an emphatic fall on "Don't" in each sentence, as in the above pattern:*

ˋDON'T start ˏ**yet,** | ˋ**will** you? / ˋDON'T make a ˏ**noise** . . . / etc.

Exercise 92. Imperatives

Note. See Exercise 90. Affirmative commands, too, can use "will you?" to make them less abrupt, but with a different intonation pattern.

Pattern: Affirmative command (Tune I): "Will you?" (Tune II.)

ˈFetch a ˋ**chair,** | ˏ**will** you?   ˈWrite it ˋ**down,** | ˏ**will** you?

Read each of the following twice or three times after the above pattern. The tag "will you?" on a rising intonation is to be used throughout—it is only printed in the first 3 examples:

ˈGo aˋ**way,** | ˏ**will** you? / ˈdo it aˋ**gain,** | ˏ**will** you? / ˈshut the ˋ**door,** | ˏ**will** you? / ˈring her ˋ**up** . . . / ˈcome ˋ**here** . . . / ˈbe ˋ**qui**et . . . / ˈmake the ˋ**toast** . . . / ˈkeep ˋ**still** . . . / ˈbuy an ˈextra ˋ**loaf** . . . / ˈturn on the ˋ**wire**less . . . / ˈhold ˋ**this** . . . / ˈlay the ˋ**tab**le . . . / ˈwater the ˋ**gar**den . . . / ˈbring me a ˋ**spoon** . . . / ˈanswer the ˋ**phone** . . . / ˈthrow it aˋ**way** . . . / ˈbrush my ˋ**coat** . . . / ˈwash the ˋ**dish**es . . . / ˈclean the ˋ**shoes** . . . / ˈbe ˋ**care**ful . . . / ˈpost this ˋ**let**ter . . . / ˈgive me a ˋ**drink** . . . / ˈbe a good ˋ**girl** . . . / ˈbe as ˈquick as you ˋ**can** . . . / ˈdo as you're ˋ**told** . . . / ˈhave another cigaˋ**rette** . . . / ˈfinish this ˋ**ex**ercise . . . / ˈmake up the ˋ**fire** . . . / ˈmend my ˋ**socks** . . . / ˈpass me the ˋ**pap**er . . . / ˈsee what the ˋ**time** is . . . / ˈbuy me a ˋ**tick**et . . . / ˈdo me a ˋ**fav**our . . .

Exercise 93. Imperatives

Note. A more friendly form of the pattern of Exercise 92 has
Tune II for the command itself (as in Exercise 89), the tag
"will you?" continuing to rise unstressed. There is scarcely
any pause between the command and the "will you?"

Pattern: Affirmative command (Tune II): "will you?"
unstressed.

| ꞏFetch a **,chair**, will you? | ꞏWrite it **,down**, will you? |

*Read the sentences of Exercise 92 according to the above
pattern:*

ꞏGo **,away**, will you? / ꞏdo it a**,gain**, will you? / ꞏshut the
,door, will you? / ꞏring her **,up**, will you? / ꞏcome **,here**, will
you? / *etc., etc.*

Exercise 94. Imperatives

Note. As in Exercise 91, the stressed form of Tune II, with a
pronounced fall on the first word, adds a feeling of personal
entreaty to the request. The tag "will you?" follows the Tune
II rise in an unstressed form as in the previous exercise.

Pattern: Affirmative command (Tune II with special
stress): "will you?" unstressed.

| `FETCH a **,chair**, will you? | `WRITE it **,down**, will you? |

*Read the sentences of Exercise 92 according to the above
pattern:*

`GO a**,way**, will you? / `DO it a**,gain**, will you ? / `SHUT the
,door, will you? / `RING her **,up**, will you? / `COME **,here**,
will you? / `BE **,qui**et, will you? / `MAKE the **,toast**, will
you? / `KEEP **,still**, will you? / *etc., etc.*

Exercise 95. Imperatives

Note. We also use the tag "won't you?" (falling intonation) with affirmative commands. The imperative itself will have Tune II. The tag "won't you?" is the normal one for the future tense: "*You will* ˋSEND me a ˏcard, | ˋwon't you?", a kind of sentence that is commonly used when we wish to be sure that the person we address does not forget something; the imperative followed by "won't you?" is similarly used as a kind of reminder.

Pattern: Affirmative command (Tune II): "Won't you?" (Tune I.)

ˈSend me a ˏcard, | ˋwon't you?

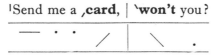

The meaning conveyed by this form of imperative is "Don't forget to send me a card!" The opening "Don't forget to . . ." can be incorporated in most of the statements of this exercise, with "will you?" as the tag.

Read each of the following twice or three times according to the above pattern. The tag "won't you?" is printed in the first three examples only, but is to be added throughout:

ˈTake ˏcare, | ˋwon't you? / ˈwrite ˏsoon, | ˋwon't you? / ˈphone me to ˏmorrow, | ˋwon't you? / ˈtell your ˏsister, . . . / ˈbe ˏquick, . . . / ˈget there in ˈgood ˏtime, . . . / ˈkeep yourself ˏwarm, . . . / ˈpost the ˏletter for me, . . . / ˈbe a ˈgood ˏboy, . . . / ˈgo to ˈbed ˏearly, . . . / ˈwrite to me ˈwhen you ˏget there, . . . / *be* ˈready to ˈleave by ˏsix, . . . / ˈlock the ˏdoor after you, . . . / ˈkeep an ˈeye on the ˏtime, . . . / ˈput the ˏlight out, . . . / ˈhold it ˏcarefully, . . . / ˈsend a ˏwire, . . . / ˈbe ˏcareful, . . . / ˈput it ˈback when you've ˏfinished, . . .

Exercise 96. Imperatives

Note. See Exercise 95. The hint of reminding the person addressed in this pattern can be further strengthened by putting special stress on the rising syllable, thus turning it into the "wave" intonation practised in earlier exercises. For "wave" intonation, see Exercises 84-88.

Pattern: Affirmative command (Stressed Tune II): "won't you?" (Tune I.)

^ISend me a ᵛCARD, | ᵛ**won't** you?

Read the sentences of Exercise 95 again with special stress on the rising intonation. Notice that the "wave" pattern may spread over more than one syllable if it is not itself the final syllable: e.g.:—

^IHold it ᵛCAREful‚ly, | ᵛ**won't** you? ^IPut the ᵛLIGHT ‚**out**, | ᵛ**won't** you? ^ILock the ᵛDOOR ‚after you, | ᵛ**won't** you? *etc.*

Exercise 97. Question-tags[1]

Note. In most languages a short stereotyped phrase replaces the variable question-tag of English. (N'est-ce pas? nicht wahr? non è vero? že-ano? зар не? не так-ли? etc. etc.) In English this conventional tag or tail varies in accordance with the verb in the remark it is added to. This next group of exercises sets out the principal uses of this device and the stress and intonation patterns associated with it.

In its simplest form the tag may be spoken on either Tune I or Tune II, the choice mainly depending on the speaker's certainty of his facts. This first exercise practises the tag on Tune I.

---

[1] Tag: literally something tied on; an appendage.

Patterns: Remark and tag both on falling intonation.

(i) *It's a* ¦fine ˋday, | ˋ**isn't** it?

(ii) *You* ¦came this ˋ**morn**ing, | ˋ**did**n't you?

This pattern is used in all remarks like (i) above where the statement is obviously true and the tag merely a polite phrase to invite the interest of the other person. It is also used as in (ii) above, where the speaker feels reasonably sure that his remark is correct and expects the listener to agree with him.

Read each of the following twice or three times according to the pattern shown:

1. ·To¦morrow's ˋ**Mon**day, | ˋ**isn't** it?
2. *You're* ¦wondering ¦who I ˋ**am**, | ˋ**aren't** you?
3. *She's* ¦quite atˋ**tract**ive, | ˋ**isn't** she?
4. *I'm* ¦rather ˋ**late**, | ˋ**aren't** I?
5. *He* ¦wasn't ¦very poˋ**lite**, | ˋ**was** he?
6. *You* ¦don't beˋ**lieve** me, | ˋ**do** you?
7. *We shall* ¦see each other aˋ**gain**, | ˋ**shan't** we?
8. *I could* ¦try aˋ**gain**, | ˋ**could**n't I?
9. *The* ¦doctor ¦came this ˋ**morn**ing, | ˋ**did**n't he?
10. *The* ¦children are at ˋ**school**, | ˋ**aren't** they?
11. *You'll* ¦stay to ˋ**tea**, | ˋ**won't** you?
12. *It* ¦looks like ˋ**rain**, | ˋ**does**n't it?
13. *We* ¦had no ˋ**choice**, | ˋ**had** we?
14. *He* ¦always has ¦lunch at ˋ**one**, | ˋ**does**n't he?
15. ¦What a ¦lovely ˋ**sun**set, | ˋ**isn't** it?
16. *You've* ¦got ˋ**brown**, | ˋ**haven't** you?
17. *You* ¦didn't ¦have to ¦wait ˋ**long**, | ˋ**did** you?
18. *She has* ¦three ˋ**chil**dren, | ˋ**hasn't** she?

19. *They were* |both `**pres**ent, | `**weren't** they?
20. *The* |wind's `**cold** today, | `**isn't** it?
21. *They* |should have `**known**, | `**should**n't they?
22. *I was* `**right**, | `**was**n't I?
23. *We must* `**hur**ry, | `**must**n't we?
24. *He* |teaches `**Eng**lish, | `**does**n't he?
25. *The* |news is at |nine o'`**clock**, | `**isn't** it?
26. *That was* |most un`**fair**, | `**was**n't it?
27. *You'll be* |free this after`**noon**, | `**won't** you?
28. *We had a* |very good `**time**, | `**did**n't we?
29. *She's a* |good `**cook**, | `**isn't** she?
30. *I* |can't |do ↑ |two things at `**once**, | `**can** I?

Exercise 98. Question-tags (continued)

Note. See previous exercise. If the tag is spoken on the rising
pattern of Tune II, we understand that the speaker is less
certain of his remark; it is presented more as a true question.
The speaker suggests: "I believe that is so, but please correct
me if I am wrong." By using this rising tag he is asking the
listener's opinion, and would not be very surprised if he were
contradicted.

Pattern: Remark (Tune I): Tag (Tune II).

> *You* |came this `**morn**ing, | ,**did**n't you?

*Read each of the following twice or three times according
to the given pattern:*

1. *It* |isn't `**sold**, | ,**is** it?
2. *You can* |drive a `**car**, | ,**can't** you?
3. *You'd* |like some `**tea**, | ,**would**n't you?
4. *You were* |late this `**morn**ing, | ,**weren't** you?
5. *We* |last |met in `**March**, | ,**did**n't we?
6. *You're* |taking the e|xam in `**June**, | ,**aren't** you?

7. *I* |ought to |give it `back, | ,oughtn't I?
8. *You* |live in `Bris`tol, | ,**don't** you?
9. *It's a* ||long |way from `here, | ,isn't it?
10. *You've* |got enough `mon`ey, | ,**haven't** you?
11. *He was* |top of his `class, | ,**wasn't** he?
12. *You* |do `smoke, | ,**don't** you?
13. *She's* `blonde, | ,isn't she?
14. *You've* for`got`ten, | ,**haven't** you?
15. *There* |won't be `room for us, | ,**will** there?
16. *The* |doctor |told you to `rest, | ,**did**n't he?
17. *He's* ||learning the vio`lin, | ,isn't he?
18. *I* |asked you be`fore, | ,**did**n't I?
19. *We could* |find out to`mor`row, | ,**could**n't we?
20. *They will* |join us `later, | ,**won't** they?
21. |Everyone a`greed, | ,**did**n't they?
22. *She'll be* |starting |school next `year, | ,**won't** she?
23. *It's* |quite im`possi`ble, | ,isn't it?
24. *He's* |got a |new `job, | ,**hasn't** he?
25. *You* |didn't `tell anybody, | ,**did** you?
26. *To*|day's the fif`teenth, | ,isn't it?
27. |No-one was `hurt, | ,**were** they?
28. *They were* |too `late, | ,**weren't** they?
29. *He can* |come `later, | ,**can't** he?
30. *There was* |no `answer, | ,**was** there?

Exercise **99** Question-tags (continued)

Note. The remarks of the two preceding exercises may also be practised in their special stress patterns; the tag remains unchanged.

Pattern: Remark (Tune I, emphatic): Tag (Tune I).

> *You came here this* `MORN`ing, | `did`n't you?

Read the following remarks from Exercise 97 in the same manner :

1. *She's quite at*ꞌTRACTive, | ꞌisn't she?
2. *It looks like* ꞌRAIN, | ꞌ**doesn't it?**
3. *I'm rather* ꞌLATE, | ꞌ**aren't I?**
4. *He teaches* ꞌENGlish, | ꞌ**doesn't he?**
5. *You're wondering who I* ꞌAM, | ꞌ**aren't you?**
6. *We shall see each other a*ꞌGAIN, | ꞌ**shan't we?**
7. *The doctor came this* ꞌMORNing, | ꞌ**didn't he?**
8. *The* ꞌDOCTor came this morning, | ꞌ**didn't he?**
9. *She has* ꞌTHREE children, | ꞌ**hasn't she?**
10. *They were both* ꞌPRESent, | ꞌ**weren't they?**
11. *They were* ꞌBOTH present, | ꞌ**weren't they?**
12. ꞌTHEY were both present, | ꞌ**weren't they?**
13. *He wasn't very po*ꞌLITE, | ꞌ**was he?**
14. *The wind's* ꞌCOLD today, | ꞌ**isn't it?**
15. *The* ꞌWIND'S cold today, | ꞌ**isn't it?**
16. ꞌHE teaches English, | ꞌ**doesn't he?**
17. *That was* ꞌMOST unfair, | ꞌ**wasn't it?**
18. *You'll be free this after*ꞌNOON, | ꞌ**won't you?**
19. *You'll be* ꞌFREE this afternoon, | ꞌ**won't you?**
20. ꞌYOU'LL be free this afternoon, | ꞌ**won't you?**

Exercise 100. Question-tags (continued)

Note. The tag on a rising tune is also unchanged if special **stress** is used in the remark.

Pattern : Remark (Tune I, emphatic): Tag (Tune II).

You came here this ꞌMORNing, | ꞋꞋdidn't you?

Read the following remarks from Exercise 98 in the same manner :

1. *You were* ˋLATE this morning, | ˏ**weren't** you?
2. *We could find out to*ˋMORrow, | ˏ**could**n't we?
3. *She'll be starting* ˋSCHOOL next year, | ˏ**won't** she?
4. *You* ˋDO smoke, | ˏ**don't** you?
5. *You* ˋCAN drive a car, | ˏ**can't** you?
6. *You're taking the exam in* ˋJUNE, | ˏ**aren't** you?
7. ˋYOU'RE taking the exam in June, | ˏ**aren't** you?
8. *The doctor told you to* ˋREST, | ˏ**did**n't he?
9. *The* ˋDOCTor told you to rest, | ˏ**did**n't he?
10. *We* ˋCOULD find out tomorrow, | ˏ**could**n't we?
11. *They'll join us* ˋLATer, | ˏ**won't** they?
12. *They* ˋWILL join us later, | ˏ**won't** they?
13. ˋTHEY'LL join us ˋLATer, | ˏ**won't** they?
14. *It's a* ˋLONG way from here, | ˏ**isn't** it?
15. *He was* ˋTOP of his class, | ˏ**wasn't** he?
16. *There won't be* ˋROOM for us, | ˏ**will** there?
17. *There* ˋWON't be room for ˋUS, | ˏ**will** there?
18. ˋHE'S got a new ˋJOB, | ˏ**hasn't** he?
19. *He can come* ˋLATer, | ˏ**can't** he?
20. ˋHE can come ˋLATer, | ˏ**can't** he?

Exercise 101. Question-tags (continued)

Note. Where the tag in Exercise 100 follows closely on the special stress there is a greater feeling of unity in the whole sentence; it might almost be considered as one unit in the emphatic form of Tune II (cf. Exercise 83). Where two special stresses are suggested (Nos. 11, 17, 18, 20), we find the whole unit takes on the pattern of a "wave intonation" over more than one syllable (Exercise 84, etc.).

The following three exercises practise the patterns produced by using Tune II in the remark itself.

Pattern: Remark (Tune II): Tag (Tune I).

You ˡdidn't ˡcome in the ˏ**morn**ing, | ˋ**did** you?

The remark itself is made more tentative by using Tune II, but the falling intonation of the tag shows that the speaker is pretty confident that his listener will not contradict.

Read each of the following twice or three times according to the given pattern:

1. ˡThis one ˡisn't ˏ**yours**, | ˋ**is** it?
2. *We* ˡneedn't ˏ**wait** for him, | ˋ**need** we?
3. *You'd* ˡlike to ˏ**speak** to him, | ˋ**would**n't you?
4. *It's* ˡnot ˡtoo ˏ**late**, | ˋ**is** it?
5. *He* ˡsaid he'd ˡcome aˏ**lone**, | ˋ**did**'nt he?
6. *You* ˡdon't ˡwant ˏ**three**, | ˋ**do** you?
7. *You* ˡwon't ˏ**mind**, | | ˋ**will** you?
8. ˡThis is the ˡone you ˏ**asked** for, | ˋ**isn't** it?
9. *You're* ˡnot ˡgoing to ˏ**cry**, | ˋ**are** you?
10. *We shall* ˡsee you toˏ**mor**row, | ˋ**shan't** we?
11. *It* ˡwasn't ˡmeant for ˏ**her**, | ˋ**was** it?
12. *He* ˡcan't ˡcome toˏ**day**, | ˋ**can** he?
13. *It's* ˡnothing to ˏ**laugh** at, | ˋ**is** it?
14. *I'm* ˡolder than ˏ**you**, | ˋ**aren't** I?
15. *It's* ˡnot the ˡsame as ˏ**mine**, | ˋ**is** it?
16. *You're* ˡnot ˡgoing to ˏ**pay**, | ˋ**are** you?
17. *She* ˡisn't ˡvery ˏ**pret**ty, | ˋ**is** she?
18. *They* ˡweren't ˏ**angry**, | ˋ**were** they?
19. ˡThis is ˏ**yours**, | ˋ**isn't** it?
20. *You'll* ˡbring it ˏ**back**, | ˋ**won't** you?

Exercise 102. Question-tags (continued)

Note. See previous exercise for general remarks. This exercise has the same pattern (Tune II) for the remark, but the **tag is** also given a rising intonation.

Pattern : Remark (Tune II) : Tag (Tune II).

You ⁱdidn't ⁱcome in the ‚**morn**ing, | ‚**did** you?

The rising tag makes the tentative remark even more uncertain; the speaker seeks the listener's assurance that his remark is correct. It is almost a real question.

Read the sentences of Exercise 101 *again, but with the tag on a rising intonation. The first 4 sentences are given below:*

1. ⁱThis one ⁱisn't ‚**yours**, | ‚**is** it?
2. *We* ⁱneedn't ‚**wait** for him, | ‚**need** we?
3. *You'd* ⁱlike to ‚**speak** to him, | ‚**would**n't you?
4. *It's* ⁱnot ⁱtoo ‚**late**, | ‚**is** it? *etc.* (see Exercise 101.)

Exercise 103. Question-tags (continued)

Note. See Exercises 101 and 102. The previous pattern is frequently found without any pause between remark and tag; the tag is not then a separate Tune II, but the unstressed rising tail of the Tune II in the remark.

Pattern : Remark (Tune II) : Tag (unstressed continuation).

You ⁱdidn't ⁱcome in the ‚**morn**ing, did you?

The effect is similar to that of the previous pattern, but the unstressed tag gives it a more casual air, as if the speaker does not wish to press the listener for his reaction to the remark.

Read the sentences of Exercise 101 *again, leaving the tag as an unstressed tail. The pause between the remark and the*

tag is negligible, the comma being merely a convention. **The**
first 4 sentences are given below:

1. ˈThis one ˈisn't **,yours**, is it?
2. *We* ˈneedn't **,wait** for him, need we?
3. *You'd* ˈlike to **,speak** to him, wouldn't you?
4. *It's* ˈnot ˈtoo **,late**, is it? *etc.* (*see Exercise* 101.)
(See Exercise 93 and 94 for a similar unstressed tag form.)

Exercise 104. Question-tags (continued)

Note. The patterns of Exercises 101 and 102 are commonly
heard with a special stress on one element of the remark. The
tags remain as before and, apart from the extra prominence given
to the stressed syllable, the complete sentence carries the same
implication as its counterpart of the earlier exercise.

Pattern: Remark (Tune II with special stress): Tag
(Tune I).

You ˋDIDn't come in the **,morn**ing, | ˋdid you?

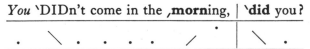

Read the sentences of Exercise 101 *again with the special
stresses suggested below. Each sentence to be read twice or
three times:*

1. ˋTHIS one isn't **,yours**, | ˋis it?
2. *We* ˋNEEDn't **,wait** for him, | ˋneed we?
3. ˋYOU'D like to **,speak** to him, | ˋwouldn't you?
4. *It's* ˋNOT too **,late**, | ˋis it?
5. *He* ˋSAID he'd come a**,lone**, | ˋdidn't he?
6. *You* ˋDON'T want **,three**, | ˋdo you?
7. ˋYOU won't **,mind**, | ˋwill you?
8. ˋTHIS is the one you **,asked** for, | ˋisn't it?
9. ˋYOU'RE not going to **,cry**, | ˋare you?
10. *We* ˋSHALL see you to**,mor**row, | ˋshan't we?
11. *It* ˋWASn't meant for **,her**, | ˋwas it?

12. 'HE can't come to,**day**, | '**can** he?
13. *It's* 'NOthing to ,**laugh** at, | '**is** it?
14. 'I'M older than ,**you**, | '**aren't** I?
15. *It's not the* 'SAME as ,**mine**, | '**is** it?
16. 'YOU'RE not going to ,**pay**, | '**are** you?
17. 'SHE isn't very ,**pret**ty, | '**is** she?
18. 'THEY weren't ,**ang**ry, | '**were** they?
19. *It* 'IS ,**yours**, | '**isn't** it?
20. 'YOU'LL bring it ,**back**, | '**won't** you?

Exercise 105. Question-tags (continued)

Note. A remark spoken in the pattern of the previous exercise can also have a Tune II tag, the whole sentence having the same background as the pattern of Exercise 102.

Pattern: Remark (Tune II with special stress): Tag (Tune II).

> *You* '**DID**n't come in the ,**morn**ing, | ,**did** you?

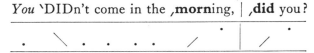

Read each of the sentences of Exercise 104 twice or three times, but with the tag on a rising intonation as in the above pattern. The first 4 sentences are given below:

1. 'THIS one isn't ,**yours**, | ,**is** it?
2. *We* 'NEEDn't ,**wait** for him, | ,**need** we?
3. 'YOU'D like to ,**speak** to him, | ,**would**n't you?
4. *It's* 'NOT too ,**late**, | ,**is** it? *etc.* (*see Exercise* 104)

Exercise 106. Question-tags (continued)

Note. As in Exercise 103, an unstressed tag is frequently used with the special stress form of Tune II practised in the previous exercise. (See note to Exercise 103.)

Pattern: Remark (Tune II, with special stress): Tag
(unstressed continuation).

> *You* `DIDn't come in the ,**morn**ing, did you?

> •   \ •   •   •   •   /   •   •   •

Repeat Exercise 104, *leaving the tag as an unstressed rising
tail. There should be scarcely any pause between the remark
and the tag.*

Exercise 107. Question-tags (continued)

Note. If the rising tone of the remark is also given special prominence, we hear once more the "wave intonation" already
practised in Exercises 84-88. The section embraced by the
"wave" carries with it some mental reservation in the mind
of the speaker; it most frequently seems to take the form of an
implied contrast.

Pattern: Remark (Tune II with special stress on rising
syllable): Tag (Tune I or II).

> *You* `DIDn't come in the `MORN,**ing**, | `**did** you?

> •   \ •   •   •   •   \/ | \ •

You `DIDn't come in the `MORN,**ing**, | `**did** you?
(I suppose you must have come in the afternoon.)

In this exercise, using the sentences of Exercise 101 once more,
the tag will sometimes be falling (Tune I) and sometimes
rising (Tune II); the rising pattern can also be read as an
unstressed tail if the teacher or reader wishes.

*Read each of the following sentences twice or three times
according to the given pattern:*

1. *This* `IS the one you `ASKED ,**for**, | `**isn't** it?
2. *You* `DON'T want ⌄THREE, | ,**do** you?
3. *It's* `NOT the same as ⌄MINE, | `**is** it?

4. *They* `WEREN'T `ANG‚ry, | ‚were they?
5. *This one* `ISn't ⌄YOURS, `is it?
6. *We* `NEEDn't `WAIT ‚fo͏ʳ him, | `need we?
7. *You'd* `LIKE to `SPEAK ‚to him, | ‚wouldn't you?
8. *It's* `NOT `TOO ‚late, | `is it?
9. *He* `SAID he'd come a⌄LONE, | `didn't he?
10. *You* `WON'T ⌄MIND, | `will you?
11. *You're* `NOT going to ⌄CRY, | ‚are you?
12. *We shall* `SEE you to`MOR‚row, | `shan't we?
13. *It* `WASn't meant for ⌄HER, | ‚was it?
14. *He* `CAN'T come to⌄DAY, | `can he?
15. *It's* `NOthing to `LAUGH ‚at, | `is it?
16. *I'm* `OLDer than ⌄YOU, | ‚aren't I?
17. *You're* `NOT going to ⌄PAY, | ‚are you?
18. *She* `ISn't very `PRET‚ty, | `is she?
19. *It* `IS ⌄YOURS, | `isn't it?
20. *You'll* `BRING it ⌄BACK, | `won't you?

Exercise 108. Question-tags (continued)

Note. The unstressed tag can replace the full Tune II form in the preceding exercise wherever it would be appropriate for the speaker to use a rising tag. (See Exercises 103 and 106.)

Pattern: Remark (Tune II with special stress on rising syllable): Tag (rising continuation of this).

You `DIDn't come in the `MORN‚ing, did you?

You `DIDn't come in the `MORN‚ing, did you?
(There is scarcely any pause between the remark and the tag.)

Repeat (from Exercise 107) Nos. 1, 2, 4, 7, 8, 11, 13, 16, and 17 in this way.

Exercise 109. Question–tags (continued)

Note. A tag in the emphatic form of Tune I is commonly used when we agree with a remark someone has just made. The "yes" or "no" of this response of agreement is normally unstressed, and, despite the conventional comma, forms a single group with the following phrase.

Pattern: (The remark we are agreeing with is between brackets).

(*You are* `EARLy this morning).    *Yes, I* `AM, | `aren't I?

(*She* ǀdidn't `see us).    *No, she* `DIDn't, | `did she?

The teacher reads the remark between brackets, the student(s) responding as shown. Each pair should be repeated at least twice:

Teacher	Student
1. (*She's a* `PRETTy ˌgirl).	
	Yes, she `IS,	`isn't she?
2. (*It* ǀlooks like `rain).	
	Yes, it `DOES,	`doesn't it?
3. (*You're* `RATHer ˇLATE).	
	Yes, I `AM,	`aren't I?
4. (*We* ǀhaven't `learnt it).	
	No, we `HAVEn't,	`have we?
5. (*It was* `HOT ˌyesterday).	
	Yes, it `WAS,	`wasn't it?
6. (*They* ǀdidn't `listen).	
	No, they `DIDn't,	`did they?
7. (*He* ǀcan't `drive).	
	No, he `CAN'T,	`can he?

8. (*They've* ˈgone aˋ**way**).

> *Yes, they* ˈHAVE, | ˋ**have**nʼt they?

9. (*I en*ˋJOY *my* ˏ**food**).

> *Yes, you* ˋDO, | ˋ**donʼt** you?

10. (*He* ˈwasnʼt ˋ**care**ful enough)

> *No, he* ˋWASnʼt, | ˋ**was** he?

11. (*We* ˈmustnʼt ˋ**break** it).

> *No, we* ˋMUSTnʼt, | ˋ**must** we?

12. (*You* ˋOUGHT *to* ˏ**know**).

> *Yes, I* ˋOUGHT (to), | ˋ**oughtnʼt** I?

13. (*Heʼs* ˈvery ˋ**kind**).

> *Yes, he* ˋIS, | ˋ**isnʼt** he?

14. (*He* ˈdid very ˈwell in his exˋ**am**).

> *Yes, he* ˋDID, | ˋ**did**nʼt he?

15. (*They have a* ˈlarge ˋ**fam**ily).

> *Yes, they* ˋHAVE, | ˋ**have**nʼt they?

16. (*She* ˈdoesnʼt ˈlook very ˋ**well**).

> *No, she* ˋDOESnʼt, | ˋ**does** she?

17. (*We* ˈmight be ˋ**late**).

> *Yes, we* ˋMIGHT, | ˋ**might**nʼt we?

18. (*The* ˈplay ˈhad a ↑ ˈgreat sucˋ**cess**).

> *Yes, it* ˋDID, | ˋ**did**nʼt it?

19. (ˈThat ˈhat doesnʼt ˋ**suit** her).

> *No, it* ˋDOESnʼt, | ˋ**does** it?

20. (*They* ˈdidnʼt ˋ**men**tion it).

> *No, they* ˋDIDnʼt, | ˋ**did** they?

21. (ˈMary was a ˈvery good ˋ**girl**).

> *Yes, she* ˋWAS, | ˋ**was**nʼt she?

22. (ˈEaster ˈcomes ↑ ˋ**ear**ly this year).

> *Yes, it* ˋDOES, | ˋ**does**nʼt it?

23. (*The* ˋSMITHS werenʼt inˏ**vit**ed).

> *No, they* ˋWEREnʼt, | ˋ**were** they?

24. (*The* ˈbabyʼs aˋ**dor**able).

> *Yes, it* ˋIS, | ˋ**isn**ʼt it?

25. (ˈJack was ˈvery unˋlucky).
　　　　　　　　Yes, he ˋWAS, | ˋwasn't he?
26. (*They* ˈdidn't ˈtake an umˋbrella).
　　　　　　　　No, they ˋDIDn't, | ˋdid they?
27. (*She* ˈcouldn't ˋhelp it).
　　　　　　　　No, she ˋCOULDn't, | ˋcould she?
28. (*They'll be* ˋANGry).
　　　　　　　　Yes, they ˋWILL, | ˋwon't they?
29. (*He* ˋSHOULDn't have left it like ˏthat).
　　　　　　　　No, he ˋSHOULDn't, | ˋshould he?
30. (*We've* ˋFINished this ˏexercise).
　　　　　　　　Yes, we ˋHAVE, | ˋhaven't we?

Exercise 110. Question-tags (continued)

Note. See previous exercise. The agreement can be made more
　emphatic by stressing the initial "yes" or "no".

Pattern:

(*She* ˈdidn't ˋsee us).　　ˋNo, | *she* ˋDIDn't, | ˋdid she?

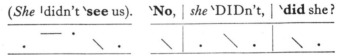

Read the examples of Exercise 109 *once more, with a
separate falling stress on each "yes" or "no".*

Exercise 111. Question-tags (continued)

Note. A similar pattern to that of the last two exercises is used for
　disbelief, sarcasm or truculence. A common response in this
　manner has an emphatic Tune I in the main response, with a
　Tune II tag. The verbs do not alternate (affirmative-negative)
　as usual, but keep the same form throughout.

Pattern: (The remark provoking the response is between
　brackets).

(*I've taken your* ˈlast ciga`**rette**).    *Oh, you* `HAVE, | ,**have** you?

(*I* ˈdon't ˈlike your `face)    *Oh, you* `DON'T, | ,**don't** you?

Students should note that, as with all these patterns where special prominence is given to any one syllable, that syllable (e.g. the falling HAVE and DON'T above) does not necessarily take a heavy **stress**. The rapid fall is its distinctive feature.

The teacher reads each remark between brackets, the student(s) responding in a disbelieving, ironical or angry fashion in the given pattern. Each pair should be spoken at least twice:

Teacher	Student

1. (*We had* ˈlunch with the `**Pres**ident).
       Oh, you `DID, | ,**did** you?
2. (*They* ˈtold me ˈall a`**bout** you).
       Oh, they `DID, | ,**did** they?
3. (*She* ˈwants to ˈsee you in `**private**).
       Oh, she `DOES, | ,**does** she?
4. (*They've* ˈtorn ˈsome of the `**pag**es).
       Oh, they `HAVE, | ,**have** they?
5. (*I was* ˈvery `**ang**ry).
       Oh, you `WERE, | ,**were** you?
6. (*She thinks you're* ˈtoo ˈlazy to `**do** it).
       Oh, she `DOES, | ,**does** she?
7. (. . . *and* ˈso do `**I**).
       Oh, you `DO, | ,**do** you?
8. (*She's* ˈeaten ˈall the `**cream**).
       Oh, she `HAS, | ,**has** she?

9. (*I'll tell* ˋMOTHer *about you*).
        Oh, you ˋWILL, | **,will** *you?*

10. (*He* ˈbroke *your* ˋgramophone *record*).
        Oh, he ˋDID, | **,did** *he?*

11. (*You* ˋSHAN'T *have it*).
        Oh, I ˋWON'T, | **,won't** *I?*

12. (*They re*ˈfused *to* ˋlisten).
        Oh, they ˋDID, | **,did** *they?*

13. (*They're* ˈgoing *with*ˋout *you*).
        Oh, they ˋARE, | **,are** *they?*

14. (ˋHE *won't* **,do** *it*).
        Oh, he ˋWON'T, | **,won't** *he?*

15. (*I'm* ˈnot ˈgoing *to* ˋtell *you*).
        Oh, you ˋAREN'T, | **,aren't** *you?*

16. (*You must* ˈdo *as I* ˋsay).
        Oh, I ˋMUST, | **,must** *I?*

17. (*She* ˋSTILL *isn't* **,ready**).
        Oh, she ˋISn't, | **,isn't** *she?*

18. (*I've* ˈleft *it at* ˋhome).
        Oh, you ˋHAVE, | **,have** *you?*

19. (*We* ˋCOULDn't **,help** *it*).
        Oh you ˋCOULDn't, | **,could**n't *you?*

20. (*They* ˈwrote ˈwhat *they* ˋthought *of you*).
        Oh, they ˋDID, | **,did** *they?*

21. (*He's* ˈwriting *a* ˋbook).
        Oh, he ˋIS, | **,is** *he?*

22. (*You're* ˈvery *un*ˋkind).
        Oh, I ˋAM, | **,am** *I?*

23. (*It's* ˋsnowing).
        Oh, it ˋIS, | **,is** *it?*

24. (*She's* ˈdyed *her* ˋhair).
        Oh, she ˋHAS, | **,has** *she?*

25. (*I'll* ˈbreak *your* ˋneck!)
        Oh, you ˋWILL, | **,will** *you?*

26. (*It's* ǀstrictly forˋ**bidd**en).
                    Oh, it ˋIS, ǀ ˏ**is** it?
27. (*He* ǀwon't ˋ**answ**er).
                    Oh, he ˋWON'T, ǀ ˏ**won't** he?
28. (*Your* ǀtrain ǀleft an ˋHOUR ago).
                    Oh, it ˋDID, ǀ ˏ**did** it?
29. (*You've got to* ˋPAY him for it).
                    Oh, I ˋHAVE, ǀ ˏ**have** I?
30. (*I* ǀthrew the ǀrest aˋ**way**).
                    Oh, you ˋDID, ǀ ˏ**did** you?

Exercise 112. Question-tags (continued)

Note. See previous exercise. This pattern can be given added emphasis by adding a falling stress to the preliminary "Oh".

Pattern: (*I've taken your* ǀlast cigaˋ**rette**)

ˋOH, ǀ *you* ˋHAVE, ǀ ˏ**have** you?

The pauses between the sections of the response are very slight.

Do Exercise 111 *again, with a falling stress on each preliminary "Oh", as shown above.*

Exercise 113. Question-tags (continued)

Note. Another common use of the question-tag device where correct intonation is important is that used when making a contrary addition to any remark. The two most usual patterns are those shown here.

Pattern: Remark (Tune I): Contrary addition (emphatic Tune II).

We ˡdidn't ˋ**meet** him, | *but* ˋHENry ˌ**did.**

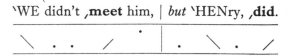

Greater contrast is suggested by using an emphatic form of Tune II in both sections.

ˋWE didn't ˌ**meet** him, | *but* ˋHENry, ˌ**did.**

The teacher reads each of the following according to the first of the above patterns, the student(s) repeating it twice after him:

1. ˡThese ˡshoes are ˡwell ˋ**made,** | *but* ˋTHOSE ˌ**aren't.**
2. *My* ˡfirst wife ˡcooked ˋ**well,** |·*but my* ˋSECond one ˌ**doesn't.**
3. ˡMilk will ˡdo you ˋ**good,** | *but* ˋBEER ˌ**won't.**
4. *He a*ˋ**greed,** | *but his* ˋWIFE ˌ**didn't.**
5. *They* ˡdon't ˋ**like** her, | *but* ˋI ˌ**do.**
6. *A* ˡfew ˡstudents didn't ˋ**work** much, | *but* ˋMOST ˌ**did.**
7. *She* ˡcouldn't underˋ**stand,** | *but* ˋHE ˌ**could.**
8. *My* ˡfriend ˡhad a ↑ ˡvery ˡdull ˋ**less**on, | *but* ˋWE ˌ**did**n't.
9. *My* ˡfather ˡnever used to ˋ**mind,** | *but my* ˋMOTHer ˌ**did.**
10. ˡWe can ˡgo ˋ**next** week, | *but* ˋTHEY ˌ**can't.**
11. *We* ˡknew her ˡvery ˋ**well,** | *but* ˋHE ˌ**did**n't.
12. ˡGrass ˡgrows very ˋ**well** here, | *but* ˋTREES ˌ**don't.**
13. ˡThey have ˡplenty of ˋ**time,** | *but* ˋWE ˌ**have**n't.

14. *The* ˈboys didn't ˈneed to ʻ**change**, | *but the* ʻGIRLS ˌ**had** to.

15. *The* ˈsmall book will ˈgo into my ʻ**pock**et, | *but the* ʻBIG one ˌ**won't**.

Exercise 114. Question-tags (concluded)

Note. See previous exercise. The form with greater contrast is quite as commonly used as the one in Exercise 113.

Pattern: See the second pattern of Exercise 113.

The teacher reads each of the following using an emphatic form of Tune II in both halves, student(s) repeating it twice after him:

1. ʻTHESE shoes are well ˌ**made**, | *but* ʻTHOSEˌ**aren't**.
2. ʻHE aˌ**greed**, | *but his* ʻWIFE ˌ**did**n't.
3. ʻSHE couldn't underˌ**stand**, | *but* ʻHE ˌ**could**.
4. *My* ʻFATHer never used to ˌ**mind**, | *but my* ʻMOTHer ˌ**did**.
5. *The* ʻSMALL book will go into my ˌ**pock**et, | *but the* ʻBIG one ˌ**won't**.
6. *My* ʻFIRST wife cooked ˌ**well**, | *but my* ʻSECond one ˌ**does**n't.
7. ʻMILK will do you ˌ**good**, | *but* ʻBEER ˌ**won't**.
8. ʻTHEY don't ˌ**like** her, | *but* ʻI ˌ**do**.
9. *A* ʻFEW students didn't ˌ**work** much, | *but* ʻMOST ˌ**did**.
10. *My* ʻFRIEND had a ʻVERy dull ˌ**less**on, | *but* ʻWE ˌ**did**n't.
11. ʻWE can go next ˌ**week**, | *but* ʻTHEY ˌ**can't**.
12. ʻWE knew her very ˌ**well**, | *but* ʻHE ˌ**did**n't.
13. ʻGRASS grows very ˌ**well** here, | *but* ʻTREES ˌ**don't**.
14. ʻTHEY have plenty of ˌ**time**, | *but* ʻWE ˌ**have**n't.
15. *The* ʻBOYS didn't need to ˌ**change**, | *but the* ʻGIRLS ˌ**had** to.

Exercise 115. Miscellaneous patterns

TYPICAL EVERYDAY TUNES AND RHYTHMS

Note. The next fifteen exercises revise this brief practical survey of the basic patterns of English stress, rhythm and intonation, by presenting hundreds of colloquial sentences and phrases as practice material based on typical patterns. These drills are best used for occasional rapid practice; they are not intended to be worked through methodically, and may be selected at random.

Hints on procedure:

Basic intonation and rhythmic pattern precede each exercise. The given rhythm is only approximate, unstressed syllables in particular being subject to slight variations in length and speed of utterance.

The syllable **da** of the syllabic rhythmic aid represents a normal stress; **di** (pronounced "dee") represents an unstressed or only partly stressed syllable.

The teacher (or leader of a group) intones the pattern twice or three times on the syllable **da** and **di** as indicated. (A glance at the first sentence or two will always make this pattern quite clear.) The group of students chant this after him three times with a well-defined rhythmic pulse.

The teacher then reads sentence 1, which is repeated by a student (or a group of students) three times in succession in a fairly regular rhythm; the teacher follows immediately with sentence 2, which a second student (or a group of students) repeats three times. Try to keep a steady rhythm running through the whole exercise.

The teacher, with very little preparation, can add further examples freely by substituting here and there other words that keep the same pattern. (Some suggestions for this are offered in the first part of Exercise 115 only.)

Pattern : ˈda di-di ˋda

ˈWhat do you ˋ**want**? (he, she, they; ˋ**do**, ˋ**hear**, ˋ**see**, etc.)

ˈIsn't it ˋ**nice**? (ˋ**hard**, ˋ**sweet**, ˋ**good**, ˋ**fast**, ˋ**smart**, ˋ**fine**, etc.)

ˈWhat will you ˋ**have**? (ˋ**do**, ˋ**take**, ˋ**say**, ˋ**write**, ˋ**see**, ˋ**drink**, etc.)

ˈQuarter past ˋ**two** (to ˋ**two**, ˋ**three**, ˋ**four**, ˋ**eight**, ˋ**nine**, etc.)

ˈGive me a ˋ**book**. (him, her, us, them; ˋ**cup**, ˋ**glass**, ˋ**pen**, ˋ**knife**, etc.)

ˈSay it aˋ**gain**. (ˈdo, ˈread, ˈbuy, ˈclean, etc; ˈpay, ˈask, ˈtell, him/her, etc.)

ˈThrow it aˋ**way**. (ˈput, ˈgive, ˈtake, ˈpush, ˈpull, etc.)

ˈYou are the ˋ**next**. (ˋ**first**, ˋ**last**, ˋ**best**. ˋ**worst**, etc.)

ˈWhat do you ˋ**say**? (ˋ**like**, ˋ**know**, ˋ**feel**, ˋ**think**, etc.)

ˈnothing at ˋ**all** / ˈstand in the ˋ**queue** / ˈwait for me ˋ**here** / ˈapples and ˋ**pears** / ˈstrawberry ˋ**jam** / ˈthanks very ˋ**much** / ˈnot in the ˋ**least** / ˈafter he's ˋ**gone** / ˈcut it in ˋ**two** / ˈdon't be too ˋ**long** / ˈsee you toˋ**night** / ˈworking all ˋ**day** / ˈnot enough ˋ**bread** / ˈcover it ˋ**up** / ˈlet's play a ˋ**game** / ˈpossibly ˋ**not** / ˈprobably ˋ**not** / ˈcertainly ˋ**not** / ˈover the ˋ**road** / ˈunder the ˋ**bed** / ˈleave it aˋ**lone** / ˈgive it to ˋ**me** / ˈnot any ˋ**more** / ˈhardly at ˋ**all** / ˈnever aˋ**gain** / ˈup to the ˋ**top** / ˈinto the ˋ**park** / ˈout of the ˋ**sun** / ˈwhen it's beˋ**gun** / ˈafter the ˋ**war** / ˈdo it aˋ**gain** / ˈcarry it ˋ**back** / ˈwalking aˋ**long** / ˈready to ˋ**start** / ˈnothing to ˋ**do** / no-ˈwhere to ˋ**go** / ˈmustn't be ˋ**late** / ˈlook at the ˋ**time** /

Exercise 116. Miscellaneous patterns

Note. See previous exercise.

Pattern: di-da di-da di-da

The ˈtrain has ˈjust come ˈin / *I* ˈdon't know ˈwhat to ˈsay / *he* ˈwants to ˈstay the ˈnight / *it's* ˈnot the ˈone I ˈwant / *I* ˈhaven't ˈheard him ˈplay / *it's* ˈjust aˈcross the ˈroad / *we* ˈcan't afˈford the ˈtime / *he* ˈsaid he'd ˈcall aˈgain / I ˈwonder ˈif he ˈwill / *he* ˈdoesn't ˈknow the ˈway / *it's* ˈtime you ˈwent to ˈwork / *you'll* ˈfind it ˈin the ˈdrawer / *I* ˈshouldn't ˈlike to ˈsay / *I* ˈdidn't ˈunderˈstand / *you* ˈmustn't ˈinterˈrupt / *we* ˈdid it ˈall aˈgain / *he'll* ˈring us ˈup at ˈeight / *I* ˈdon't beˈlieve you ˈcan / *I* ˈreally ˈthink you ˈought / *I* ˈwonder ˈif it's ˈlate / *I* ˈnever ˈhave the ˈtime / *he* ˈtold me ˈwhere to ˈgo / *you* ˈleft them ˈon the ˈshelf / *you* ˈput them ˈthere yourˈself / *re*ˈmember ˈwho he ˈis / *my* ˈhusband's ˈnot at ˈhome / *I* ˈdon't know ˈwho to ˈask / *I* ˈdon't know ˈwhere to ˈgo / *I'd* / ˈlike to ˈhave the ˈsame / *I'd* ˈrather ˈyou reˈmained / *you'd* ˈbetter stay at ˈhome / *we* ˈcouldn't ˈquite aˈgree / *it* ˈisn't ˈquite the ˈsame / *it's* ˈnot as ˈgood as ˈyours / *I* ˈdoubt if ˈshe will ˈknow / *it's* ˈcoming ˈon to ˈrain / *there's* ˈplenty ˈmore to ˈdo / *it's* ˈall the ˈsame to ˈme / *a* ˈlovely ˈbunch of ˈflowers / *she* ˈisn't ˈon the ˈphone / *there's* ˈnothing ˈleft to ˈsell / *it's* ˈtime to ˈgo to ˈbed.

Exercise 117. Miscellaneous patterns

Note. See Exercise 115.

Pattern: ˈda-di ˌda di

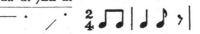

ᴵAre you ˌ**cert**ain? / ᴵwill you ˌ**need** one? / ᴵwait a ˌ**mo**-ment / ᴵcan you ˌ**see** him? / ᴵdo you ˌ**like** it? / ᴵdid you ˌ**know** him? / ᴵthat's the ˌ**spir**it! / ᴵI can ˌ**hear** you / ᴵare we ˌ**ear**ly? / ᴵhave you ˌ**seen** him? / ᴵshall we ˌ**take** one? / ᴵif you ˌ**want** to / ᴵjust a ˌ**mo**ment / ᴵget a ˌ**move** on! / ᴵcome aˌ**long**, then / ᴵwill you ˌ**ask** him / ᴵwould you ˌ**like** to? / ᴵsix-and-ˌ**eight**pence? / ᴵare you ˌ**hung**ry? / ᴵmust you ˌ**real**ly? / ᴵcan you ˌ**man**age? / ᴵhas it ˌ**stopped** yet? / ᴵdoes it ˌ**mat**ter? / ᴵmind the ˌ**door**step! / ᴵdid you ˌ**hear** me? / ᴵare they ˌ**bet**ter? / ᴵhow's your ˌ**fath**er? / ᴵdid she ˌ**prom**ise? / ᴵdo be ˌ**care**ful! / ᴵhave aˌ**noth**er? / ᴵdid he ˌ**kiss** you? / ᴵafter ˌ**din**ner? / ᴵcan I ˌ**take** one? / ᴵdo you ˌ**think** so / ᴵis he ˌ**up** yet? / ᴵdid they ˌ**like** it? / ᴵlike to ˌ**taste** one? / ᴵsee you ˌ**lat**er.

The first of the two stresses in the above pattern is normally the weaker. In fairly rapid conversation this stress would disappear, leaving two unstressed syllables at a fairly high pitch, viz:

Read some of the phrases from Exercise 117 again, beginning with two high unstressed syllables as suggested above.

Exercise 118. Miscellaneous patterns

Note. See Exercise 115.

Pattern: ᴵda ˌ**da**-di-di

ᴵI'll ˌ**wait** for you / ᴵdon't ˌ**wait** for us / ᴵdon't ˌ**worry** her! / ᴵeat ˌ**half** of it! / ᴵwe'll ˌ**see** to it / ᴵcome ˌ**back** again! / ᴵwrite ˌ**fre**quently! / ᴵnext ˌ**Sat**urday! / ᴵnear **Self**-ridge's? / ᴵjust ˌ**opp**osite? / ᴵnot ˌ**read**y yet? / ᴵthey ˌ**want**-

ed to? / ˈwe'll ˌ**answ**er them / ˈby ˌ**tele**phone? / ˈnew
ˌ**fur**niture? / ˈyour ˌ**grand**mother? / ˈon ˌ**hol**iday? / ˈpicked
ˌ**yes**terday? / ˈhe's ˌ**off**ered to? / ˈmy ˌ**aut**ograph? / ˈwhole-
ˌ**heart**edly?

Exercise 119. Miscellaneous patterns

Note. See Exercise 115. For notes on repeated questions see
Exercise 73.

Pattern: ˌ**da** di-di da

The last syllable may be partially stressed on a rising intonation.

It is one of the commoner patterns used for repeated or doubtful questions.

what was his name? / ˌ**which** was the way? / ˌ**when** was it
done? / ˌ**were** they all right? / ˌ**what** did you pay? / ˌ**who** was
the man? / ˌ**where** did you stay? / ˌ**why** was he late? / ˌ**where**
have they been? / ˌ**when** did you go? / ˌ**when** must you leave?
/ ˌ**what** did you say? / ˌ**must** it be now? / ˌ**who** did you see?
/ ˌ**was** it too late? / ˌ**what** did she do? / ˌ**would** it be right?
ˌ**did** they obey? / ˌ**who** was to blame? / ˌ**was** he in time? /
ˌ**not** with the hand? / ˌ**half** of us can?

Exercise 120. Miscellaneous patterns

Note. See Exercise 115.

Pattern: di-ˋ**DA** di-da

Of ˋCOURSE you can / *he* ˋTOLD me so / *I* ˋKNOW you
will / *there* ˋISn't one / *you* ˋCAN'T have been / *e*ˋNORM-

ously / *I* 'HAVEn't one / *we* 'GAVE them some / *to*-
'MORrow night / *on* 'SATurday / *they're* 'NOT for me /
he's 'SURE to come / *oh*, 'CERTainly / *per*'HAPS he will
/ *I've* 'FINished it / *he* 'WASn't there / *it's* 'TERRible /
they're 'EVerywhere / *it* 'CAN'T be true / *an* 'EXtra one
/ *you've* 'BROKen it / *the* 'LEFT-hand one / *you* 'MUST
have known / *you* 'OUGHT to know / *you* 'OUGHT to
have / *he* 'CAN'T have known / *he* 'COULDN'T have
known / *he* 'COULDn't have / *we've* 'LENT them all /
I'd 'RATHer not / *you're* 'ALways late.

Exercise 121 Miscellaneous patterns

Note. See Exercise 115.

Pattern: di-di 'DA di

absoˈLUTEly / *that's what* 'WE said / *for the* 'MOment
/ *just for* 'PRACTice / *on the* 'BLACKboard / *when the*
'TRAIN comes / *in the* 'EVEning / *I'm a*'FRAID so / *if
you* 'WANT to / *contra*'DICtion / *on the* 'CORNer / *in
the* 'COUNtry / *at the* 'SEAside / *as I* 'TOLD you / *but
you* 'OUGHT to / *when I* 'HAVE to / *as we* 'USED to /
we must 'PAY them / *they will* 'ASK you / *I'd be* 'GRATE-
ful . . . / *I should* 'LIKE to / *they've a*'GREED to / *I
ar*'RANGed it / *what's he* 'UP to? / *on the* 'OFF-chance
/ *no, of* 'COURSE not / *yes, I'd* 'LOVE to / *yes, I* 'MEANT
to / *that's what* 'WE thought.

Exercise 122. Miscellaneous patterns

Note. See Exercise 115.

Pattern: di 'DA-di-di ,da

(*The preliminary unstressed syllable is optional.*)

We 'KNOW it's not ,**right** / *you* 'TOLD me to ,**ask** / 'JUST for a ,**while** / *I'd* 'LIKE you to ,**come** / 'WHO do you ,**mean**? / . . . *if* 'THAT'S what you ,**want** / *it's* 'NEVer too ,**late** / 'ASK him a,**gain** / *I* 'KNOW what she ,**wants** / *I* 'WASn't sur,**prised** / *it's* 'TIME you be,**gan** / 'HOW could you ,**tell**? / *you* 'NEVer can ,**tell** / *it* 'USED to be ,**there** / *I* 'THOUGHT it was ,**late** / *I'll* 'TRY to be ,**good** / *you* 'MUST have a ,**drink** / *it's* 'TIME they were ,**paid** / *they* 'WANTed to ,**help** / *it's* 'BEST to be ,**frank** / . . . *for a* 'MINute or ,**two** / *he* 'SAID he would ,**come** / *they* 'ASKED me to ,**phone** / . . . *well it* 'OUGHTn't to ,**be** / *he* 'DIDn't ob,**ject** / *there* 'WASn't much ,**time** / *I* 'KNEW it would ,**fail** / *I* 'WISH I were ,**rich** / *there's* 'NO-one in ,**sight** / *if* 'ONly I'd ,**known**.

Exercise 123. Miscellaneous patterns

Note. See Exercise 115.

Pattern: 'DA di ,**da**

'WE don't ,**mind** / 'THAT'S O.,**K.** / 'SHE won't ,**know** / 'WAIT a ,**bit** / 'HERE I ,**am** / 'THEY don't ,**know** / 'HERE'S a ,**knife** / 'AFTer ,**you** / . . . (*but*) 'MARy ,**does** / 'THAT'S e,**nough** / 'THAT won't ,**do** / 'THAT'S no ,**use** / 'BE a ,**sport**! / 'WE don't ,**care**! / 'HALF will ,**do** / 'NEVer ,**mind**! / 'YOURS is ,**best** / 'TAKE some ,**more** / 'THEY won't ,**know** / 'HERE'S a ,**piece** / 'THERE you ,**are** / 'THAT'S the ,**one** / 'NOT like ,**that** / 'NOW'S the ,**time**! / 'THIS one's ,**yours** / 'HERE you ,**are**! / 'THAT'S the ,**way** / 'HAVE a ,**heart**! (= don't be severe!) / 'DO be ,**quick**! / 'VERy ,**well**! / 'STRANGE to ,**say** . . . / (*it's* 'QUITE all

,right / ‘I won’t ,tell / ‘RIGHT you ,are! (= certainly!) /
‘NOW and ,then / ‘ONE or ,two / ‘THAT’S not ,right /
‘YOU can ,come / ‘MINE’S all ,right.

Exercise 124. Miscellaneous patterns

Note. See Exercise 115.

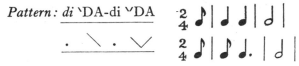

Pattern: di ‘DA-di ⌄DA

(For introductory exercises on the “wave” intonation used
here, see Exercises 84 to 87.)

you ‘CAN’T be ⌄SURE / *I’d* ‘LOVE to ⌄TRY / *they* ‘CAN’T
have ⌄LEFT / *it* ‘ISN’t ⌄BAD / *it’s* ‘NOT for ⌄YOU / *I*
‘THINK she ⌄WILL / *now* ‘DON’T be ⌄LATE / *you*
‘MUST have ⌄KNOWN / *it’s* ‘NOT the ⌄SAME / *it’s* ‘FAR
too ⌄SOON / *I’d* ‘LIKE to ⌄KNOW / *it’s* ‘QUITE all
⌄RIGHT / *we* ‘KNEW they ⌄WOULD / *it* ‘ISn’t ⌄MINE
/ *I* ‘HOPE I ⌄SHALL / *we* ‘OUGHT to ⌄GO / *you’re*
‘VERy ⌄KIND / *he’s* ‘VERy ⌄STRICT / *she’s* ‘VERy ⌄SWEET
/ *I* ‘HOPE you ⌄DID / *we* ‘ASKED him ⌄TWICE / *you*
‘MUSTn’t ⌄CRY / *it’s* ‘TWELVE o’⌄CLOCK / *they* ‘TRIED
to ⌄HELP / *he* ‘SAID he’d ⌄COME / *he* ‘THINKS he
⌄CAN / *it’s* ‘NOT to⌄NIGHT / *it* ‘MUST be ⌄STAMPED
/ *he’s* ‘JUST the ⌄SAME / *she* ‘WON’T be ⌄PLEASED
/ *we* ‘TRIED to ⌄PHONE / *you* ‘SAID he ⌄WAS /
I ‘HEARD they ⌄DID / *I* ‘THOUGHT I ⌄COULD /
you ‘KNOW you ⌄CAN’T / *he* ‘NEVer ⌄SMILES / *you*
‘OUGHT to ⌄GO / *it’s* ‘ONly ⌄ONE / *it’s* ‘QUITE
⌄eNOUGH / *we* ‘CAN’T to⌄DAY / *it’s* ‘ALL we’ve ⌄GOT /
you’ll ‘HAVE to ⌄TRY / *it’s* ‘BETter ⌄NOW / *I* ‘WISH
you’d ⌄SAY (=tell me) / *he* ‘HOPES you’re ⌄WELL / *it’s*
‘TIME to ⌄GO / *it’s* ‘MUCH too ⌄DEAR / *it* ‘CAN’T be

ᵛHELPED / *you* ʿMUST be ᵛQUICK / it's ʿHARD to
ᵛFIND / he ʿHASn't ᵛPAID / *they* ʿCAN'T have ᵛGONE
/ *I* ʿHOPE you ᵛWILL / *I* ʿWISH he ᵛWOULD / *he*
ʿWON'T be ᵛTHERE.

Exercise 125. Miscellaneous patterns

Note. See Exercise 115. The pattern used in this exercise is most
commonly found as a response suggesting a doubtful or
critical attitude towards a remark that has been made. When
a verb is involved, the form used is one of the question-tag
patterns isolated from its remark, which is of course that of
the first speaker.

Pattern: ˌ**da** di

$$\frac{2}{4} \left| \; \downarrow \quad \flat \quad \gamma \right|$$

ˌmust I? / ˌdid you? / ˌare they? / ˌdoes he? / ˌcan we?
/ ˌdo they? / ˌshould I? / ˌshall we? / ˌcould it? / ˌmay
I? / ˌcan't she? / ˌdon't they? / ˌshan't I? / ˌwill he?
/ ˌreally? / ˌwon't they? / ˌtruly? / ˌought we? / ˌwho
was? / ˌwhy not? / ˌSunday? / ˌis it? / ˌhave they? /
ˌhad she? / ˌmight I? / ˌaren't I? / ˌweren't you? / ˌhalf
past? / ˌsixpence? / ˌafter? / ˌwould you? / ˌalways? / ˌpar-
don? / ˌwas it? / ˌwon't they? / ˌwho did? / ˌyou did?
/ ˌoh?

Exercise 126. Miscellaneous patterns

Note. See Exercise 115, also note after Exercise 117 on the
alternative stress of the pattern used in that exercise.

Pattern: ⁻*di-di* ˌ**da**

$$\frac{2}{4} \left| \; \sqcap \; \right| \left| \; \downarrow \; \gamma \; \right|$$

This pattern is the usual one for short "yes-no" questions;
the first syllable has lost its stress to give more point to the

significant rising stress, but it still retains its high pitch. Note
the printed sign used above for an unstressed initial syllable on
a high pitch.

⁻do you ,**mind**? | ⁻is that ,**right**? | ⁻can you ,**come**? | ⁻if
you ,**like** | ⁻not at ,**all** | ⁻was she ,**there**? | ⁻is he ,**here**?
| ⁻are you ,**tired**? | ⁻have some ,**more**? | ⁻on the ,**right**? |
⁻half an ,**hour**? | ⁻did you ,**know**? | ⁻are you ,**sure**? |
⁻over ,**there**? | ⁻may I ,**see**? | ⁻will you ,**write**? | ⁻have
you ,**time**? | ⁻can I ,**phone**? | ⁻after ,**tea**? | ⁻was it
,**nice**? | ⁻he's a ,**what**? | ⁻have a ,**drink**? | ⁻near the
,**bank**? | ⁻is it ,**safe**? | ⁻fifty ,**two**? | ⁻does it ,**work**? | ⁻in
the ,**spring**? | ⁻for a ,**bet**? | ⁻did you ,**win**? | ⁻at the ,**top**?
| ⁻can you ,**swim**? | ⁻have a ,**go**? | ⁻have you ,**heard**? |
⁻even ,**now**? | ⁻for a ,**week**? | ⁻by her,**self**? | ⁻two by
,**two**? | ⁻am I ,**wrong**?

Exercise 127. Miscellaneous patterns

Note. See Exercise 115.

Pattern: `DA di ⌄DA

The first fall in this pattern is scarcely noticed with short
closed syllables, since the vowel is too short to be heard gliding
down. The pattern then sounds more like

The differene ccan be clearly heard in:

`YOU'RE the ⌄NEXT          `THIS one's ⌄YOURS

and

As they are, however, both subjectively the same, the
emphatic fall will always be used in print: `YOU'RE the
⌄NEXT. `THIS one's ⌄YOURS.

ˋDON'T ask ˅ME / ˋCOME back ˅SOON / ˋBRING it ˅BACK / ˋPLEASE don't ˅WAIT / ˋTHAT'S not ˅MINE / ˋTHIS one's ˅YOURS / ˋYOU'RE the ˅NEXT / ˋYOU should ˅KNOW / ˋHAVE a ˅HEART! / ˋDON'T be ˅LATE / ˋWAIT for ˅ME / ˋPLEASE be ˅QUICK / ˋMIND your ˅HEAD / ˋDON'T eat ˅MINE / ˋHE'S no ˅FOOL / (*it's*) ˋTIME to ˅START / (*it*) ˋLOOKS like ˅SNOW / ˋDON'T be ˅LONG / ˋNOT just ˅NOW.

See also Exercise 96 for more imperatives using this pattern.

Exercise 128. Miscellaneous patterns

Note. See Exercise 115.

Pattern: di-ˋda, | ˏda-di-di-(di).

—and similar rhythms according to the number of syllables.

This pattern is the usual one for remarks followed by a hesitant or qualifying afterthought (see Exercise 62). As the division of the statement into two sections becomes less marked, so the intonation pattern gradually takes on the more continuous quality of Tune II with special stress (see example at the end of this exercise).

they ˋ**might,** | *on the* ˏ**oth**er hand. // *He's* ˋ**right,** | ˏ**I** should say. // *You* ˋ**can,** | ˏ**afterwards.** // *I* ˋ**know** | *what the* ˏ**oth**ers do. // *I'll* ˋ**come,** | *if you* ˏ**want** me to. // *He's* ˋ**late,** | ˏ**gen**erally. // *I* ˋ**can't** | ˏ**Saturdays.** // *I* ˋ**walk,** | *as a* ˏ**rule.** // *It's* ˋ**his,** | ˏ**prob**ably. // *You're* ˋ**wrong,** | ˏ**actually.** // *I* ˋ**had** one | ˏ**yesterday.** // *It's* ˋ**bad,** | ˏ**cand**idly. // *He* ˋ**lived** here | ˏ**form**erly. // *I'll* ˋ**come,** | *if the* ˏ**oth**ers do.

The only difference between this pattern and the type shown in Exercise 83 is in the length of the pause that follows the falling intonation. Many of the above can easily be imagined as single units of an emphatic Tune II.

I `had one, | ‚**yes**terday.   *I* `HAD one ‚**yes**terday.

The element of contrast or doubt is still present (in the rising intonation). Fact and objectivity are shown by using Tune I only:

I ˈhad one `**yes**terday.

Exercise 129. Miscellaneous patterns

Note. See Exercise 115. The stressed form of Tune II mentioned at the end of the previous exercise is most appropriate for expressions of apology and regret.

Pattern: di-`DA ‚**da**-di.

(. . .and variants with added unstressed syllables.)

I'm `SO ‚**sorry** / *I* `MUST a‚**pol**ogize / *it was* `MY mis‚**take** / `DO ex‚**cuse** *us* / *we* `DO hope you'll for‚**give** *us* / *I* `BEG *your* ‚**pard**on / *I* `DIDn't ‚**mean** *to* / . . . *so* `PLEASE for‚**give** *me* / *I* `COULDn't ‚**help** *it* / *I'm* `VERy ‚**sorry** / *it was* `MY ‚**fault** / *it* `WAS ‚**care**less of me / *how* `COULD I be so ‚**silly** / *it was* `OUR ‚**fault** / *I've* `SUCH a bad memory for ‚**faces.**

Exercise 130. Miscellaneous patterns

Note. See Exercise 115. A falling intonation is normally used for short-form answers to "yes-no" questions.

Pattern: (ˈCan you ‚**come**?)   *Yes, I* `**can**.   *No, I* `**can't**.

Exercise 132. Miscellaneous patterns

Note. The short helping-verb response to a question-word question is usually spoken with an emphatic form of Tune I.

Pattern: (ˈWhich ˈanimals ˈlive ˋ**long**est?)   ˋTORtoises do.

The teacher reads the question between brackets, the student(s) answering according to the given pattern:

1. (ˈWho came ˋ**late**?)
     ˋNObody did.
2. (ˈWhich of us may ˋ**have** a piece?)
     You ˋBOTH may.
3. (ˈWhich kind of ˈbook ˋ**in**terests you?)
     *A de*ˋTECTive story does.
4. (ˈWho is ˋ**com**ing tonight?)
     My aunt and ˋUNCle are.
5. (ˈWhich of you have ˋ**books**?)
     We ˋALL have.
6. (ˈWhich of them can ˈspeak ˋ**French**?)
     They ˋBOTH can.
7. (ˈWho's ˈtaken my ˋ**pen**?)
     ˋ**I** have.
8. (ˈWhat ˈanimal ˈlikes ˋ**milk**?)
     A ˋCAT does.
9. (ˈWho ˋ**saw** you?)
     ˋNObody did.
10. (ˈWho wrote ˈParadise ˋ**Lost**?)
     ˋMILton did.
11. (ˈWhose ˈhomework ˈwasn't ˋ**done**?)
     ˋMINE wasn't.
12. (ˈWhich of you can ˈdo this ˋ**exercise**?)
     We ˋALL can.

13. (ˈWho ˈbroke the ˈ**wind**ow?)

ˈHE did.

14. (ˈWho will ˈvolunˈ**teer**?)

ˈWE will.

15. (ˈWho ˈheard the ˈ**broad**cast?)

Nearly ˈEVerybody did.

16. (ˈWho has ˈbeen here beˈ**fore**?)

ˈTHOSE two have.

17. (ˈWhich ˈanimal has a ˈgood ˈ**mem**ory?)

The ˈELephant has.

18. (ˈWhich of you ˈchildren ˈspilt the ˈ**ink**?)

ˈNONE of us did.

19. (ˈWho ˈhas to go ˈ**early**?)

ˈWE have (do, must).

20. (ˈWhat ˈday is ˈ**best** for you?)

ˈTUESday is.

Exercise 133. Miscellaneous patterns

Note. See Exercise 109. The agreement response is often heard without its complementary tag. In this form it shows less interest in the subject that is spoken about; it is more detached, casual and non-committal. It is exactly the same pattern as that of Exercise 130, but is used in a different situation.

Pattern: (*It's a* ˈlovely ˈ**day** today).   *Yes, it* ˈ**is**.

The teacher makes the remark between brackets, the student(s) agreeing with it. Both remark and agreement to be repeated if the latter is not satisfactory:

1. (*It's a* ˈlovely ˈ**day** today).

Yes, it ˈ**is**.

2. (*They* ˈdidn't ˈ**take** it).

No, they ˈ**didn't**.

3. (*I shall be* `**late**).

    Yes, you `**will**.

4. (*She* |doesn't look `**well**).

    No, she `**does**n't.

5. (*You've* |finished `**early**).

    Yes, I `**have**.

6. (*I* |see you |don't ꜜSMOKE).

    No, I `**don't**.

7. (*He was* |very up`**set**).

    Yes, he `**was**.

8. (*We must* `**hur**ry).

    Yes, we `**must**.

9. (*You* `COULD do `BET,ter).

    Yes, I `**could**.

10. (*He* |ought to see a `**doc**tor).

    Yes, he `**ough**t (`**did**).

11. (*She* |looked `**love**ly).

    Yes, she `**did**.

12. (*He's* |passed his |final ex`**am**).

    Yes, he `**has**.

13. (*You* |need a `**hair**cut).

    Yes, I `**do**.

14. (*Her* |father |didn't ap`**prove**).

    No, he `**did**n't.

15. (*They've been* |very `**lucky**).

    Yes, they `**have**.

Exercise 134. Miscellaneous patterns

Note. The agreement pattern of the previous exercise is made a little more definite by speaking the "yes" or "no" on a falling intonation.

Pattern: (*It's a* |lovely `**day** today).    `**Yes**, | *it* `**is**.

Do Exercise 133 again in this more definite form.

Finally, do Exercise 109 in the pattern of Exercise 133 or 134; and do Exercise 133 in the question-tag pattern of Exercise 109.

Exercise 135. Miscellaneous patterns

Note. See Exercise 115. We very commonly agree with some remark, but are surprised that it is true. This element of the unexpected is expressed by using a response beginning with a high unstressed "so + pronoun" device.

Pattern: (*You've* ˈdropped your ˋ**glove**).

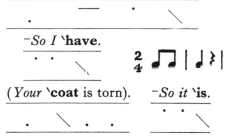

−*So I* ˋ**have**.

(*Your* ˋ**coat** is torn). −*So it* ˋ**is**.

The teacher reads the remark between brackets in the pattern shown, the student(s) adding the surprised agreement. If repetition is necessary, both remark and agreement should be repeated:

1. (*The* ˈsun's ˈsetting alˋ**ready**).

    −*So it* ˋ**is**.

2. (*You* ˋPROMised to ˏ**do** it).

    −*So I* ˋ**did**.

3. (*We could* ˈtie it with ˋ**string**).

    −*So we* ˋ**could**.

4. (*You've* ˈburnt the ˈtoast aˋ**gain**).

    −*So I* ˋ**have**.

5. (*They were* ˈall ˋ**mine**).

    −*So they* ˋ**were**.

6. (*I* `ALways said he was ,**right**).

                                     –*So you* `**did.**

7. (*He was our* |first `**pres**ident).

                                     –*So he* `**was.**

8. (`**Oh!** | *We've for*|gotten to `**thank** him).

                                     –*So we* `**have.**

9. (*We can* |pick him up `**lat**er).

                                     –*So we* `**can.**

10. (*They've* |fallen on the `**floor**).

                                     –*So they* `**have.**

11. (*She's* |changed her `**hair**-style).

                                     –*So she* `**has.**

12. (*We shall have* |been |here a `**WEEK** to,**mor**row).

                                     –*So we* `**shall.**

13. (*He* `SAID it would ,**rain**).

                                     –*So he* `**did.**

14. (*They'll be* `HERE ,**soon**).

                                   –*So they* `**will.**

15. (*She was* `LATE ,**yes**terday).

                                   –*So she* `**was.**

16. (*You're* |eating the |paper, ↑ `**too**).

                                   –*So I* `**am.**

17. (*You've* |drunk my `**beer**).

                                   –*So I* `**have.**

18. (*That's the* `SECond time you've done ,**that**).

                                   –*So it* `**is.**

19. (*I drank* `YOUR beer by mistake `LAST ,**week**).

                                 –*So you* `**did.**

20. (`**Look!** | *It's* `**snow**ing).

                                 –*So it* `**is.**

21. (*He* |usually has |lunch at `**home**).

                                 –*So he* `**does.**

22. (*I was the* `FIRST to finish to,**day**).

                                 –*So you* `**were.**

23. (*You could* ˈcome in the ˋ**morn**ing).

        –*So I* ˋ**could.**

24. (*They've* ˈbought a ˈnew ˋ**car**).

        –*So they* ˋ**have.**

25. (*We can* ˈget ˈback by ˋ**boat**).

        –*So we* ˋ**can.**

Exercise 136. Miscellaneous patterns

Note. When contradicting someone we use the same grammatical form that we use when we agree with them (Exercise 133) or when we answer a "yes-no" question (Exercise 130). The only difference lies in the intonation pattern. An emphatic form of Tune II is used for contradiction.

Pattern: (*You're* ˋ**late**).   ˋNO, I'm ˏ**not.**

(*I* ˈcan't ˋ**do** it).   ˋYES, you ˏ**can.**

N.B. There is **no pause** after the YES or NO, the comma being merely a convention.

The teacher reads each of the following remarks between brackets, the student(s) contradicting in the above pattern. If repetition is necessary, both remark and contradiction should be repeated:

1. (*I've* ˈnever ˋ**heard** of it).

        ˋYES, you ˏ**have.**

2. (*I've got* ˋMORE than ˏ**you**).

        ˋNO, you ˏ**haven**'t.

3. (*You were* ˋTOLD a,**bout** it).

        ˋNO, we ˏ**weren**'t.

4. (*It's* ˋNOT ˇYOURS).

        ˋYES, it ˏ**is.**

5. (*It's* ˈnot ˋthere).

ˋYES, it ˌis.

6. (*You* ˋALways obˌject).

ˋNO, I ˌdon't.

7. (*He* ˈcan't ˋdo it).

ˋYES, he ˌcan.

8. (*They* ˋNEVer do what I ˌsay).

ˋYES, they ˌdo.

9. (*I* ˈthink it was ˋblue).

ˋNO, it ˌwasn't.

10. (*He* ˈwasn't inˋvited).

ˋYES, he ˌwas.

11. (*The* ˈbooks ˈweren't ˋthere).

ˋYES, they ˌwere.

12. (*She's* ˈgone aˋway).

ˋNO, she ˌhasn't.

13. (*You* ˈmust have ˋburnt it).

ˋNO, I ˌdidn't.

14. (*You* ˈweren't at ˋhome).

ˋYES, I ˌwas.

15. (*I* ˋCOULD have ˌdone it).

ˋNo, you ˌcouldn't.

16. (*You're* ˈvery ˋselfish).

ˋNO, I'm ˌnot.

17. (*They* ˈdidn't ˋbring any).

ˋYES, they ˌdid.

18. (*She's* ˈfound a ˈnew ˋjob).

ˋNO, she ˌhasn't.

19. (*The* ˈchildren ˈdidn't ˋgo).

ˋYES, they ˌdid.

20. (*They* ˈwon't ˋlend me one).

ˋYES, they ˌwill.

21. (*We* ˋDIDn't ˌmean to).

ˋYES, you ˌdid.

22. (*You're* |not `quick enough).

    `YES, I ,am.

23. (*We could* `GET there in an ,hour).

    `NO, we ,couldn't.

24. (*He'll* |give you a `new one).

    `NO, he ,won't.

25. (*The* `OTHers haven't `COME yet).

    `YES, they ,have.

26. (`I wasn't ,there).

    `YES, you ,were.

27. (*You'll* `drop it).

    `NO, I ,shan't.

28. (*He* |didn't `finish it).

    `YES, he ,did.

29. (*She's* |left |school at `last).

    `NO, she ,hasn't.

30. (*They're* |not `ready).

    `YES, they ,are.

31. (`THAT won't ,help you).

    `YES, it ,will.

32. (`HE knows ,best).

    `NO, he, ,doesn't.

33. (*He* |can't `come).

    `YES, he ,can.

34. (*He* |won't a`gree).

    `YES, he ,will.

35. (*She* |knows al`ready).

    `NO, she ,doesn't.

Exercise 137. Miscellaneous patterns

Note. "Fairly" and "rather" in contrasting phrases. These two words are used to qualify adjectives and adverbs. They mean "to a certain extent", but "fairly" is used with a feeling of approval and "rather" with a sense of disapproval or disparagement. So we should talk of the children being "rather naughty" and "fairly good"; and our soup is "fairly hot" or "rather cold". If we say the soup is "rather hot" we are suggesting that it is too hot to eat. A child may be "fairly tall for his age", meaning he is quite a fine, well-built child; if we say he is "rather tall for his age" we suggest he is too tall, taller than he ought to be, he is perhaps outgrowing his strength. The two ideas are often used for contrast in the course of conversation, and are normally heard in the patterns suggested below. (The use of these two words is more complicated than this, for "rather" is also used with approval in phrases like "I think that's rather clever of me", or the exclamation ˋRA˅THER! In this exercise we shall confine ourselves to the basic contrast mentioned above.)

Patterns:

When used in isolated phrases where no contrast is implied, Tune I is normal.

ˈMy ˈroom is ˈfairly ˋ**large.**   ˈMy ˈroom is ˈrather ˋ**small.**

When contrast is implied, we normally use special stress to mark the contrasting elements, the "fairly" section being with Tune II and the "rather" section with Tune I.

ˋMY room is fairly ˌ**large,** |

but ˋYOUR room's rather ˋSMALL.

Even when these ideas occur separately, they are normally spoken with the pattern given above:

ˈLet's ˈhave the ˈmeeting ˋ**here**—ˋMY room's fairly ˌ**large.**

We must ˈmeet ˈsomewhere ˈelse—ˈMY room's rather ˈSMALL.

"Pretty" can replace either of these words; "somewhat" can replace "rather".

The teacher reads each part of the following "fairly—rather" contrasts, the student(s) repeating that part twice after him. The same student (or group of students) should practise both parts:

1. ˈYOUR apple's fairly ˌripe. ˈTHIS apple's rather ˈGREEN.
2. ˈTHIS pencil's fairly ˌsharp. ˈTHAT pencil's rather ˈBLUNT.
3. ˈTHIS light is fairly ˌbright. ˈTHAT light is pretty ˈDIM.
4. ˈMY tea's fairly ˌhot. ˈHER tea's rather ˈCOLD.
5. ˈHE lives fairly ˌnear. ˈWE live rather ˈFAR.
6. ˈTHAT one is fairly ˌthick. ˈTHIS one is rather ˈTHIN.
7. ˈMY books are fairly ˌnew. ˈYOUR books are rather ˈOLD.
8. ˈYOUR hands are fairly ˌclean. ˈHER hands are rather ˈDIRTy.
9. ˈSOME of them are fairly ˌkeen, | *but* ˈMOST of them are rather ˈDULL.
10. ˈHE'S pretty ˌlively. ˈI'M rather ˈTIRED.
11. ˈTHIS pear's fairly ˌsoft. ˈTHAT one's rather ˈHARD.
12. ˈYOUR house is fairly ˌlarge. ˈMY house is rather ˈSMALL.
13. ˈSHE is pretty ˌquick. ˈHE is somewhat ˈSLOW.
14. ˈTHIS textbook is fairly ˌgood. ˈTHAT book is rather ˈPOOR.

15. `YOUR coffee's fairly ,**strong**.  `MY coffee's rather `WEAK.

Sometimes special stress is heard on the words "fairly" and "rather" in sentences like those above.

`THIS pencil's fairly ,**sharp**.   (Quite sharp.)

`THIS pencil's `FAIRLY ,**sharp**.   (Apologetic; I hope it will do.)

`MY house is rather `SMALL.   (I wish it were larger.)

`MY house is `RA,**ther** `SMALL.   (Apologetic; I do hope you understand why I can't invite you all.)

Exercise 138. Miscellaneous patterns

Note. This exercise and the following one practise the two intonations of the phrase "I thought you did" and its variants. This phrase is a common one as a response to both an expected and an unexpected answer to a question.

Pattern (for an expected reply).

A. *You* `**knew** him, | ,**did**n't you?   B. `Y**es**.

A. *I* `THOUGHT you ,**did**.

The student(s) should read the question and make the response, the teacher merely adding the necessary "yes" or "no", indicated by Y or N. If there is any difficulty at first, the teacher can read the student's part to help him, the student repeating it immediately after him:

1. *Is* ¹this your ,**first** visit?
         (Y)   *I* `THOUGHT it ,**was**.
2. *I'm* ¹not `**late**, | ,**am** I?
         (N)   *I* `THOUGHT I ,**was**n't.

3. ˈDid you ˈget my ˌmessage?
          (Y)   I ˈTHOUGHT you ˌdid.
4. ˈMust we ˈpay at the ˌdoor?
          (Y)   I ˈTHOUGHT we ˌhad to.
5. ˈWere you at the ˌlecture?
          (Y)   I ˈTHOUGHT you ˌwere.
6. ˈDid you ˈgo to the ˌlecture?
          (Y)   I ˈTHOUGHT you ˌdid.
7. ˈCan you ˈspeak ˌFrench?
          (Y)   I ˈTHOUGHT you ˌcould.
8. ˈMust we ˈshow our ˌtickets?
          (Y)   I ˈTHOUGHT we ˌhad to.
9. ˈDo you ˈtake ˌsugar?
          (Y)   I ˈTHOUGHT you did.
10. ˈWould you ˈlike to ˌmeet him?
          (Y)   I ˈTHOUGIIT you ˌwould.
11. ˈWill you be ˈseeing him to,ˈmorrow?
          (Y)   I ˈTHOUGHT you ˌwould.
12. ˈShall I ˈknow your ˈanswer ˌsoon?
          (Y)   I ˈTHOUGHT I ˌshould.
13. ˈHave they ˈbrought our ˌbooks back?
          (Y)   I ˈTHOUGHT they ˌhad.
14. ˈWill you be ˈthere to,ˈmorrow?
          (Y)   I ˈTHOUGHT you ˌwould.
15. *Is* ˈthat the ˈTown ˌHall?
          (Y)   I ˈTHOUGHT it ˌwas.
16. ˈCan we ˈleave it ˌhere?
          (Y)   I ˈTHOUGHT we ˌcould.
17. ˈDid he reˈturn your ˌbook?
          (Y)   I ˈTHOUGHT he ˌwould
18. ˈWere they ˈtelling the ˌtruth?
          (Y)   I ˈTHOUGHT they ˌwere.
19. ˈDid she acˈcept the ˌpresent?
          (Y)   I ˈTHOUGHT she ˌwould.

20. ¹Have they ex¹plained ‚everything?
          (Y)   *I* ʽTHOUGHT they ‚**had.**

21. *Is* ¹that the ¹one you ‚**want**?
          (Y)   *I* ʽTHOUGHT it ‚**was.**

22. ¹Can he ¹under‚**stand** us?
          (Y)   *I* ʽTHOUGHT he ‚**could.**

23. ¹Shall I ¹hear the re¹sults ‚**soon**?
          (Y)   *I* ʽTHOUGHT I ‚**should.**

24. ¹Did you ¹mean what you ‚**said**?
          (Y)   *I* ʽTHOUGHT you ‚**did.**

25. ¹Were the ¹children ‚**with** you?
          (Y)   *I* ʽTHOUGHT they ‚**were.**

26. ¹Was that a ¹knock at the ‚**door**?
          (Y)   *I* ʽTHOUGHT it ‚**was.**

27. ¹Will you be ¹able to ‚**help**?
          (Y)   *I* ʽTHOUGHT you ‚**would.**

28. ¹Has my ¹letter been ‚**posted**?
          (Y)   *I* ʽTHOUGHT it ‚**had.**

29. ¹Can she ¹play ‚**chess**?
          (Y)   *I* ʽTHOUGHT she ‚**could.**

30. *You* ʽDIDn't ʽWANT ‚**it**, | ‚**did** you?
          (N)   *I* ʽTHOUGHT you ‚**did**n't.

31. ¹Have you been ¹waiting ‚**long**?
          (Y)   *I* ʽTHOUGHT you ‚**had.**

32. ¹Need we ‚**wait**?
          (N)   *I* ʽTHOUGHT we ‚**need**n't.

33. ¹Does it ¹need a ¹2½d.* ‚**stamp**?
          (Y)   *I* ʽTHOUGHT it ‚**did.**

  * twopenny-halfpenny (¹tʌpni-¹heipni).

34. *This* ¹meat is ʽ**bad**, | ‚**isn't** it?
          (Y)   *I* ʽTHOUGHT it ‚**was.**

35. *The* ʽMILK'S not ‚**sour**, | ʽ**is** it?
          (N)   *I* ʽTHOUGHT it ‚**was**n't.

36. ˈWas I ˌ**right**?
>   (Y)   *I* ˈTHOUGHT I ˌ**was**.
37. *You* ˈcan't ˋ**come**, | ˋ**can** you?
>   (N)   *I* ˈTHOUGHT you ˌ**could**n't.
38. ˈHas the ˌ**post** arrived?
>   (Y)   *I* ˈTHOUGHT it ˌ**had**.
39. ˈHave you ˈtold her the ˌ**news**?
>   (Y)   *I* ˈTHOUGHT you ˌ**had**.
40. ˈDo you ˌ**want** me?
>   (Y)   *I* ˈTHOUGHT you ˌ**did**.

Exercise 139. Miscellaneous patterns

Note. See Exercise 138.

Pattern: (for an unexpected reply).

>   A. *You* ˋ**knew** him, | ˌ**did**n't you?   B. ˋ**No** or ˌ**No**

>   B. ⁻*I* ˌ**thought** you ˋDID.

The rise that begins on ˌ**thought** is scarcely noticed until we hear the unstressed "you" on a higher tone. Being a syllable closed with a voice-less consonant its chief characteristic is its low pitch after the initial unstressed but fairly high-pitched pronoun.

The student(s) should read the question and make the response, the teacher merely answering the question with the "yes" or "no", shown by (Y) or (N) in the exercise:

1. *Is* ˈthis your ˌ**first** visit?
>   (N)   ⁻*I* ˌ**thought** it ˋWAS.
2. *I'm* ˈnot ˋ**late**, | ˌ**am** I?
>   (Y)   ⁻*I* ˌ**thought** I ˋWASn't.

3. ˈDid you ˈget my ˌ**mess**age?
(N)   ⁻I ˌ**thought** you ʽDID.

4. ˈMust we ˈpay at the ˌ**door**?
(N)   ⁻I ˌ**thought** we ʽHAD to.

5. ˈWere you at the ˌ**lect**ure?
(N)   ⁻I ˌ**thought** you ·WERE.

6. ˈDid you ˈgo to the ˌ**lect**ure?
(N)   ⁻I ˌ**thought** you ʽDID.

7. ˈCan you ˈspeak ˌ**French**?
(N)   ⁻I ˌ**thought** you ʽCOULD.

8. ˈMust we ˈshow our ˌ**tick**ets?
(N)   ⁻I ˌ**thought** we ʽHAD to.

9. ˈDo you ˈtake ˌ**sug**ar?
(N)   ⁻I ˌ**thought** you ʽDID.

10. ˈWould you ˈlike to ˌ**meet** him?
(N)   ⁻I ˌ**thought** you ʽWOULD.

11. ˈWill you be ˈseeing him toˌ**mor**row?
(N)   ⁻I ˌ**thought** you ʽWOULD.

12. ˈShall I ˈknow your ˈanswer ˌ**soon**?
(N)   ⁻I ˌ**thought** I ʽSHOULD.

13. ˈHave they ˈbrought our ˌ**books** back?
(N)   ⁻I ˌ**thought** they ʽHAD

14. ˈWill you be ˈthere toˌ**mor**row?
(N)   ⁻I ˌ**thought** you ʽWOULD.

15. *Is* ˈthat the ˈTown ˌ**Hall**?
(N)   ⁻I ˌ**thought** it ʽWAS.

16. ˈCan we ˈleave it ˌ**here**?
(N)   ⁻I ˌ**thought** we ʽCOULD.

17. ˈDid he reˈturn your ˌ**book**?
(N)   ⁻I ˌ**thought** he ʽDID.

18. ˈWere they ˈtelling the ˌ**truth**?
(N)   ⁻I ˌ**thought** they ʽWERE.

19. ˈDid she acˈcept the ˌ**pres**ent?
(N)   ⁻I ˌ**thought** she ʽWOULD.

20. ˈHave they exˈplained ˌeverything?
                    (N)   ‾I ˌthought they ˋHAD.
21. *Is* ˈthat the ˈone you ˌwant?
                    (N)   ‾I ˌthought it ˋWAS.
22. ˈCan he ˈunderˌstand us?
                    (N)   ‾I ˌthought he ˋCOULD.
23. ˈShall I ˈhear the reˈsults ˌsoon?
                    (N)   ‾I ˌthought I ˋSHOULD
24. ˈDid you ˈmean what you ˌsaid?
                    (N)   ‾I ˌthought you ˋDID.
25. ˈWere the ˌchildren with you?
                    (N)   ‾I ˌthought they ˋWERE.
26. ˈWas that a ˈknock at the ˌdoor?
                    (N)   ‾I ˌthought it ˋWAS.
27. ˈWill you be ˈable to ˌhelp?
                    (N)   ‾I ˌthought you ˋWOULD.
28. ˈHas my ˈletter been ˌposted?
                    (N)   ‾I ˌthought it ˋHAD.
29. ˈCan she ˈplay ˌchess?
                    (N)   ‾I ˌthought she ˋCOULD.
30. *You* ˈdidn't ˋWANT it, | ˌdid you?
                    (Y)   ‾I ˌthought you ˋDIDn't.
31. ˈHave you been ˈwaiting ˌlong?
                    (N)   ‾I ˌthought you ˋHAD.
32. ˈNeed we ˌwait?
                    (Y)   ‾I ˌthought we ˋNEEDn't.
33. ˈDoes it ˈneed a ˈ2½d. ˌstamp?
                    (N)   ‾I ˌthought it ˋDID.
34. *This* ˈmeat is ˋbad, | ˌisn't it?
                    (N)   ‾I ˌthought it ˋWAS.
35. *The* ˋMILK'S not ˌsour, | ˋis it?
                    (Y)   ‾I ˌthought it ˋWASn't.
36. ˈWas I ˌright?
                    (N)   ‾I ˌthought I ˋWAS.

37. *You* ˈcan't ˈ`come, | ˈcan you?
        (Y)   ⁻*I* ˌ**thought** you ˈCOULDn't.

38. ˈHas the ˌ**post** arrived?
        (N)   ⁻*I* ˌ**thought** it ˈHAD.

39. ˈHave you ˈtold her the ˌ**news**?
        (N)   ⁻*I* ˌ**thought** you ˈHAD.

40. ˈDo you ˌ**want** me?
        (N)   ⁻*I* ˌ**thought** you ˈDID.

Exercise 140. Miscellaneous patterns

Note. See Exercise 138 and 139.

Pattern:

A. *You* ˈ**knew** him, | ˌ**did**n't you? B. (i) ˈ**Yes.** (ii) ˈ**No.**

A. (i) *I* ˈTHOUGHT you ˌ**did.** (ii) ⁻*I* ˌ**thought** you ˈDID.

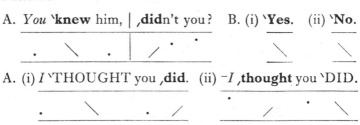

The student reads any question from the preceding exercise. The teacher answers "Yes" or "No" at random, and the student must respond with the correct intonation pattern.

Exercise 141. Prose dialogue

Note. Many foreign students find it difficult to read English prose in dialogue form in a natural manner. The mistake usually lies in the wrong reading of the passages that connect the actual dialogue. These passages usually begin with "he said/he asked, etc." and are to be considered merely as interpolations or stage "asides". The preceding section of dialogue dictates the movement of the explanatory passage of prose that follows it. This passage is always more or less weakly stressed, and its intonation follows in the same direction as the last stress of the dialogue itself.

Pattern: (For Tune I).

"*You* ꞁcan't ꞌ**come**", he said angrily.

There is no appreciable rise in the voice after the significant fall on "come", the following descriptive part merely being treated as an unstressed "tail".

The teacher reads each of the following short fragments of dialogue as indicated, the student(s) repeating it twice after him:

1. " ꞁWhat's it ꞌ**for**?" he inquired in a whisper.
2. " *You'll* ꞁhave to ꞁput a ꞌ**stamp** on," he explained in his best French.
3. " ꞁNot for ꞌ**sale**," proclaimed the notice in the window.
4. "*It's* ꞁtime for ꞌ**bed**," he said with a yawn.
5. "*I* ꞁdon't ꞌ**know**", he said quietly.
6. " ꞁCome ꞌ**here!**" she ordered in a sharp voice.
7. "*It* ꞁisn't ꞌ**mine**," he said for the second time.
8. " ꞁGive it to ꞌ**me**," she said with a smile.
9. " *You've* ꞁdropped it on the ꞌ**floor**," he complained to her.
10. "*We* ꞁdidn't ꞌ**ask** him," they explained briefly.
11. " *The* ꞁnext one's ꞁnumber ꞌ**ten**," he said rather pointlessly.
12. " *You should have* ꞁtold me beꞌ**fore**," he complained bitterly.
13. " *But you* ꞁdidn't ꞌ**ask** me," was the prompt reply.
14. " *They* ꞁmust have forꞌ**got**ten," John said to himself.
15. " *We'll* ꞁfinish with ꞌ**this** one," she said closing the book.

Exercise 142. Prose dialogue (continued)

Note. See Exercise 141 for general remarks. When the actual dialogue has a Tune II intonation pattern, the final rise continues as a "tail" of unstressed syllables, also rising.

Pattern: (For Tune II).

" ꟾCan you ˌ**come**?" he asked, quietly.

There is no further fall in the voice after the rise on "come" in the dialogue, but the following syllables are more or less unstressed.

The teacher reads each of the following short fragments of dialogue as indicated, the student(s) repeating it twice after him:

1. "*Is* ꟾthis for ˌ**me**?" he asked with surprise.
2. "*I* `HOPE you don't ˌ**mind**," she remarked apologetically.
3. " ꟾShall we ˌ**ask** him to?" they whispered to one another.
4. "*I'm* `GLAD you ˌ**came**," she said as they left.
5. "*Do you* `REALly ˌ**think** so?" she said excitedly.
6. "*It's the* `BEST we can ᵛDO," he explained to them.
7. " ꟾDid you ˌ**meet** him?" she inquired at once.
8. " ꟾPlease ˌ**take** one," she said invitingly.
9. " ꟾDo you ꟾthink it's ˌ**true**?" they kept on asking.
10. " ꟾWould you ꟾlike a ˌ**drink**?" he said with a smile.
11. "*It's* `NICE of you to ᵛASK," he said with a shake of his head.
12. " ꟾWill you ˌ**wait** for me?" she called from upstairs.
13. "*It's* ꟾnot so ˌ**bad**," he admitted at last.
14. " ꟾWill you ꟾsend it by ˌ**post**?" he asked her.
15. " ꟾCan you ꟾcome aˌ**gain**?" she added as an afterthought.

Exercise 143. Prose dialogue (continued)

Note. See Exercises 141 and 142. The unstressed "tails" in the last two exercises were fairly short. As they get longer we can feel the rhythm of their original stressed forms more clearly. This has already been noted before in Exercise 67, but the phenomenon is even more strongly marked in these conversation readings. The next two exercises offer longer examples for practice.

Pattern: (Tune I).

When the unstressed tail is fairly long, the pattern of the original rhythm is more distinctly felt; in particular, the last stress of the tail will attempt to sink even lower than the normal low level to which the end of the actual dialogue has already fallen. We shall show this tendency in the exercises by using italics for the "tail", and a special accent, viz: ˌsaid, for the low partial stresses. The final stress, which tends to fall still further, will be printed in heavier type: aˌ**way**.

" *You* ˈcan't ˋ**come**," he ˌ*said* ˌ*slowly turning a*ˌ***way***.

The teacher reads each of the following fragments of dialogue in the manner indicated, the student(s) repeating it once or twice after him:

1. " ˈCome ˋ**here**!" *com*ˌ*manded the* ˌ*captain in a* ˌ*loud* ˌ***voice***.
2. "*It's* ˈnearly ˈten oˋ**clock**," *she ob*ˌ*served,* ˌ*glancing at her* ˌ***watch***.
3. " *You've for*ˈgotten your ˋ**bag**," *he* ˌ*said with a* ˌ***smile***.
4. " ˈWhat a ˋ**pi**ty!" *was* ˌ*all I* ˌ*said when he* ˌ*broke a* ˌ***glass***.
5. " ˈPass the ˋ**but**ter!" *she de*ˌ*manded,* ˌ*stretching out her* ˌ***hand***.

6. "*I* ˈthink it's ˈgoing to ˋ**rain**," *he re*ˌ*marked, looking* ˌ*up at the black* ˌ**sky**.

7. " ˈHave aˋ**nother** one," *he* ˌ*begged as he* ˌ*offered me the* ˌ**box**.

8. " ˈQuite ˋ**right**"! *he* ˌ*added,* ˌ*nodding his* ˌ**head**.

9. "ˋ**Show** me!" *requested the* ˌ*little man in the* ˌ*bowler* ˌ**hat**.

10. "*I must* ˈput some ˋ**coal** on the fire," *she re*ˌ*marked getting* ˌ*up from her* ˌ**chair**.

11. "ˋ**Yes**, | *it's a* ˈvery good ˋ**film**," *he a*ˌ*greed* ˌ*settling himself* ˌ**com**fortably.

12. "*I* ˈdon't beˋ**lieve** it," *he re*ˌ*plied in a firm* ˌ**tone**.

13. " ˈThat's ˈnot the ˋ**point**," *I* ˌ*argued in face of* ˌ*strong oppo-*ˌ**sition**.

14. "*I* ˈdon't ˋ**know**," *she* ˌ*answered,* ˌ*looking* ˌ**puzz**led.

15. "*Be* ˈback in ˈhalf an ˋ**hour**," *she* ˌ*reminded him* ˌ**stern**ly.

16. "*We* ˈreally ˈmust be ˋ**go**ing now," *she* ˌ*said,* ˌ*getting up* ˌ*out of her* ˌ**chair**.

17. "*I've* ˈnearly ˋ**fin**ished it!" *he ex*ˌ*claimed with a note of* ˌ**pride** *in his voice*.

18. "*You've made the* ˈsame misˈtake aˋ**gain**!" *the teacher com*ˌ*plained with a* ˌ**frown**.

19. "*No, I* ˋ**can't**!" *she re*ˌ*plied,* ˌ*shaking her* ˌ**head**.

20. "*I* ˈdisaˋ**gree**," *said the* ˌ*next speaker,* ˌ*rising to his* ˌ**feet**.

21. "ˋ**Stop** it!" *shouted the little* ˌ*girl to her* ˌ**broth**er.

22. "*I* ˋ**KNOW** that!" *she* ˌ*said, turning a*ˌ*way in an*ˌ**noy**-ance.

23. "*Of* ˋ**COURSE**!" *he re*ˌ*torted rather* ˌ**rude**ly.

24. "*It's* ˈnot ˋ**poss**ible," *was the o*ˌ*pinion he* ˌ*offered after a* ˌ*moment's* ˌ**thought**.

25. " ˈPleased to ˋ**meet** you," *he* ˌ*said,* ˌ*holding out his* ˌ**hand**.

26. "*It's* ˈrather exˋpensive," *she* reˌmarked, ˌlooking *in the shop* ˌwindow.

27. "*With* ˋpleasure!" *he* ˌsaid, ˌbowing *to her like a* ˌcavalier *of* ˌold.

28. "ˈOver ˋthere!" *he said to his* ˌfriend *with a wave of his* ˌhand.

29. "ˈWhat was ˋthat?" *he* ˌasked, ˌholding *up a finger for* ˌsilence.

30. "ˈThis is ˋyours!" *he* reˌmarked ˌhanding *me the* ˌbrown *one.*

Exercise 144. Prose dialogue (continued)

Note. See Exercises 142 and 143. This exercise contains longer "tails" to a dialogue ending on the rising pattern of Tune II.

Pattern: The pattern of the normally stressed rhythm is evident also in longer "tails" of a rising type, and again the last stress of all tries to rise even higher after the manner of a normal significant stress. We shall show this behaviour in the practice material by printing the "tail" in italics, placing an accent before the syllables that tend to regain a partial stress (ˈasked), and by printing the final stress, which shows a tendency to rise even more steeply, in heavier type (ˈ**door**). This final partial stress may perhaps be considered as an echo of the significant-stress rise or fall of the dialogue that precedes it.

ˈCan you ˌ**come**? *he* ˈasked ˈquietly *closing the* ˈ**door.**

The teacher reads each of the fragments of dialogue in the manner indicated, the student(s) repeating it once or twice after him:

1. "ˈDid you ˌ**hear**?" *he* reˈpeated *with an* ˈangry ˈ**frown.**

2. "ˈIs that ˌ**you**?" *he* ˈcalled *as the* ˈ**door** *banged.*

3. " ˈAre you ˌready?" he ˈasked in an imˈpatient ˈtone.

4. " ˈDo you ˌlike it?" she ˈasked, ˈshowing off her ˈnew ˈdress.

5. " ˈPass the ˌsugar, please," she ˈsaid in a ˈvoice just as ˈsweet.

6. " ˈAren't you ˌwell?" her mother ˈasked, looking ˈdoubtfully ˈat her.

7. " It's ˋHARDly ˇFAIR," I obˈjected, when I ˈsaw what had ˈhappened.

8. " ˈMind ˈhow you ˇGO," she ˈwarned as he ˈset out in the ˈsnow.

9. " ˈDo you ˌdrink?" she ˈasked, ˈlooking at him seˈverely.

10. " ˈHave they ˌgone?" he inˈquired in an ˈanxious ˈvoice.

11. " ˈAre you ˌsure?" he ˈasked, looking aˈround him as he ˈspoke.

12. " Is ˈthat eˌnough?" she ˈasked as she ˈpassed his ˈplate.

13. " It's ˋJUST as ˇWELL," she ˈsaid with an inˈdignant ˈtoss of her ˈhead.

14. " ˈMay I ˌjoin you?" he ˈasked as he apˈproached the ˈtable.

15. " ˉOn ˌThursday?" he sugˈgested, ˈtaking out his ˈdiary.

16. " ˈShall we ˈtake a ˌtaxi?" she ˈasked, ˈlooking at the ˈpouring ˈrain.

17. " ˋI don't ˌmind," my ˈmother said with a ˈsmile.

18. " We're ˈnot ˋlate, | I ˌhope," I ˈasked, as my ˈhostess came ˈforward to ˈmeet us.

19. " D'you ˈmind my ˈopening the ˌwindow?" he inˈquired, ˈglancing around the ˈroom.

20. " ˈAre you aˌsleep?" she ˈasked, ˈtiptoe-ing ˈover to his ˈchair.

21. " ¹Is the ˏwater hot yet?" *he* deˈmanded, ˈpoking his ˈhead round the ˈ**door**.

22. " ¹Do you ˈreally ˏ**want** to?" *she* inˈquired, as he ˈtook the ˈbaby ˈ**from** her.

23. " ¹Have you ˈgot the reˏ**ceipt**?" *he* ˈasked, as she was ˈcounting her ˈ**change**.

24. " ¹Would you ˈlike a ˏ**drink**?" *he* ˈasked as he ˈled her to the ˈ**bar**.

25. " ¹Do you ˈstill ˏ**love** me?" *he* ˈwhispered, his ˈarm ˈstealing round her ˈ**waist**.

26. " *Was* ˈthat the ˏ**door**bell?" *he* ˈasked, not atˈtempting to ˈ**move**.

27. " *Is* ˈthat all ˏ**right**?" *she* ˈasked, ˈshowing him the ˈ**lett**er.

28. " *It's* ˈall the ˈsame to ˅ME," *he* ˈsaid, ˈshrugging his ˈ**should**ers.

29. " ˈThe ˋKETTle's ˏ**boil**ing," *he* ˈshouted from the ˈ**kitch**en.

30. " ˋTHAT'S the ˏ**house**," *he* ˈsaid, ˈpointing across the ˈroad to the ˈbungalow with the ˈdoor painted ˈbright ˈ**blue**.

Exercise 145. Prose dialogue (continued)

Note. See Exercises 141 to 144. This exercise practises short sequences of dialogue with both forms of unstressed "tail" following the passage between quotation marks.

The teacher reads each sentence of the dialogue fragments separately according to the given intonation pattern, the student(s) repeating it once or twice after him:

1. " *Now* ˈwho can ˈtell me the ˈname of ˋ**this** country?" *asked the* ˌteacher, with ˌone finger on the ˌ**map**.
    "ˋI ˏ**can!** " *said little* ˈJohnny, ˈsitting in the ˈfront ˈ**row**.
    " ˈWhat ˋ**is** it?" *she went* ˌon, smiling ˌ**down** at him.

"'**Chi**na," *he re*ˌ*plied with a* ˌ*self-satisfied* ˌ**look** *on his face.*

2. "'**Tick**ets, please!" *called the at*ˌ*tendant as they* ˌ*entered the* ˌ**hall**.

"'YOU'VE got them, ˌ**have**n't you, Emily?" *asked Miss* ˈ**Green** ˈ*fumbling in her* ˈ**bag**.

"'**Yes**, | *of* 'COURSE!" *her* ˌ*friend answered,* ˌ*handing them to the at*ˌ**tend***ant.*

" ˈThis ˌ**way**, please," *he* ˈsaid, ˈ*going on a* ˈ**head** *of them.*

3. " ˈStand ˈby to ˌlower the '**boats**!" *he* ˌshouted, *as a* ˌ*nother wave* ˌ*broke over the* ˌ**deck**.

" ˈWomen and ˈchildren ˌ**first**!" *the captain* ˈordered *as he* ˈstruggled *to hold the* ˈ**wheel**.

" ˈAre there any ˌ**more**?" *bawled the* ˈmate, ˈstanding *in the* ˈladen ˈboat be ˈ**low**.

"'**No**. ˈLet her 'go!" *came the re*ˌply, *almost* ˌdrowned *by the* ˌ*whistling of the* ˌ**wind**.

4. " *And* ˈhow are '**you** today?" *smiled the* ˌdoctor, ˌ*entering the* ˈ*little girl's* ˌ**room**.

" ˈAll ˌ**right**, thank you," *she* ˈfaltered, ˈ*looking at him* ˈ**timidly**.

" ˈOpen your ˌ**mouth**!" *he said,* ˈ*bending over her* ˈ**bed**.

" ˈNow say '**Ah**!" *he added, as he* ˌ*peered down her* ˌ**throat**.

" ˈDo you ˈthink she's ˌ**bett**er, doctor?" *asked the* ˈ**moth**er. "*Or* ˈmust she ˈgo to '**hosp**ital?"

" *She'll* ˈbe all ˈright in a ˌ**day** *or two," the doctor* re ˈplied *with an en* ˈcouraging ˈ**smile**.

5. " ˈLet's go and ex ˈplore the ˅**CAVES**!" *suggested* ˈDavid, ˈ*getting up off the* ˈsand, *where he'd been lying* ˈ*basking in the* ˈ**sun**.

" *I'm* ˈtoo '**sleep**y," *grumbled* ˌ**Joan**, ˌ*stifling a* ˌ**yawn**.

"'COME ˌ**on**!" *he* ˈurged, ˈ*pulling her by the* ˈ**arm**.

" ˈAll ˌ**right**!" *she* ˈsaid, *brushing the* ˈ*sand off her* ˈ**clothes**.

"*But* ╵hadn't we ╵better tell ˌ**Moth**er?" *she added,*
╵*looking across towards the row of* ╵*deck-chairs*
where the ╵*grown-ups were* ╵*taking their* ╵*afternoon*
╵*nap.*

"*Oh,* ʽSHE won't ˌ**mind.** ʽRACE you there!" *shouted*
ˌ*David setting off at* ˌ*top* ˌ**speed.**

6. "ʽFAˌ**ther,** | ╵will you ˌ**carve**?" *asked Mother,* ╵*bustling*
round with the ╵*veg*etable *dishes.*

"ʽ**Cert**ainly, my dear," *he* ˌ*answered,* ˌ*rolling up his*
ˌ*sleeves.*

" ╵Wash your ˌ**hands,** children!" *Mother* ╵*called,*
sitting the ╵*baby in his* ╵*high* ╵*chair.*

" ╵Don't ˌ**wait**!" *shouted the* ╵*twins,* ╵*running in later*
with ╵*hungry* ╵*looks.*

" ╵Are they ˌ**clean**?" *she de*╵*manded,* ╵*looking at them*
su╵**spic**iously.

"*I* ʽTHOUGHT ˌ**not**! *You'll* ╵have to ╵wash them
a*ʽ*gain!" *she said firmly,* ˌ*pushing them* ˌ**out.**

"*Is* ╵that e,**nough** for you, dear?" *asked her* ╵*husband,*
╵*passing up a* ╵*plate.*

"*It's* ╵just ʽ**right**," *she replied,* ˌ*piling some po*ˌ*tatoes*
beside the ˌ**meat.**

7. "*Ex*ʽCUSE ˌ**me,** | *but* ╵does this ╵bus ╵go to Tra╵falgar
ˌ**Square**?" *asked a* ╵*well-dressed* ╵*man, po*╵*litely*
raising his ╵*bowler-*╵**hat.**

"*Yes, it* ʽ**does**," *answered a young* ˌ*lady waiting in the*
ˌ*queue.*

" ╵Hurry a,**long** there!" *shouted the con*╵*ductor,* ╵*bending*
down to ╵*help up a small* ╵*child.*

" ╵Any more ˌ**fares,** please?" *he went* ╵*on, as the* ╵*bus*
started ╵**up** *again.*

" ╵Two ʽ**six**pennies, please," *said an old* ˌ*lady, holding*
a ˌ*shopping basket on one* ˌ*arm and her* ˌ*grandchild on*
her ˌ**lap.**

"'nk ˌ**you**," *said the* conˈ**ductor** *as he gave her her* ˈ**change**.

" *Tra*ˈfalgar ˋ**Square**, *please*," *said the* ˌ**man** *in the* ˌ**bowler**, ˌ**holding** *out a* ˌ**ten-shilling** ˌ**note**.

" ˈ**Haven't** *you any* ˌ**change**?" *asked the* conˈ**ductor**, ˈ**feeling** *in his* ˈ**bag**.

8. " ˈ**Would** *you like a*ˈ**nother** *piece of* ˌ**pie**?" *the landlady's daughter* ˈ**asked** *him, smiling* ˈ**coyly** *at him over the* ˈ**top** *of the* ˈ**pie**-dish.

"ˋ**NO**!" *he answered at* ˌ**once**, *with the* ˌ**look** *of a hunted* ˌ**animal** *in his* ˌ**eyes**.

" ˈ**Are** *you* ˌ**sure**?" *she asked a*ˈ**gain**, ˈ**taking** *up the* ˈ**knife** *as she* ˈ**spoke**.

" *Well per*ˈhaps *just a* ˋ**litt**le," *he* ˌ**murmured**, *his* ˌ**glance** *torn between the* ˌ**knife** *in her hand and the* ˌ**glint** *in her* ˌ**eye**.

Specimen of continuous prose dialogue
MUM'S THE WORD

"*I've* ˈcome *up to* ˋ**talk** *to you*," *my mother said,* | "'ˈwhile *you're getting* ˋ**READ**y. ˈWho's ˈgoing *to* ˈbe *at the* ˋ**par**ty?"

"*I* ˈdon't ˋ**know**," *I said.*

" ˈWill *you* enˌ**joy** *it*?" *my mother asked.*

" ˋ**I** ˌ**hope** *so*," *I said.*

"*You've* ˈonly *got* ˈfifteen ˋ**MIN**ˌ**utes**," *my mother said.*

"*Yes, I* ˋ**know**."

"*Can I* ˌ**help** *you*?" *my mother asked.*

" ˋ**No**, | *thanks* ˌ**aw**fully," *I said.*

" ˈWill ˌ**Betty** *be there*?"

" ˋ**No**," *I said.*

" ˈWhy ˋ**not**?"

"*Because the* `peo*ple giving the* `par*ty don't* `KNOW *her.*"

" `THAT'S ˏfunny," *my mother said.* "*I* 'wonder `why *they don't.* 'Isn't that `fun*ny, their* 'not `*knowing her?*"

" `Why?"

" `Well, | *because it* `IS," *my mother said.* "*Why don't you* intro`DUCE *her to them? They'd* `like *her.* `I'VE ˏal*ways liked Betty. I was* 'telling your 'father the ↑ `OTHer ˏday | *that I've* 'always liked `Bet*ty.* 'What are you 'rubbing `on?"

"*Foun*`da*tion cream," I said.*

"*I'm glad* `I *don't have to do all* ⌄THAT," *my mother said.*

" `YOU *use* ˏpow*der.*"

"*I don't* `BOTHer *with all that* `OTHer *old* ˏrub*bish," my mother said.* "*My* `POW*der only blows* `OFF | `any*way. I* `LIKE *that* ˏdress. *It* `suits *you. It* 'doesn't 'make *you look* ↑ `old | *and* `hag*gard* | *like* `SOME *of the things you* ˏwear. 'That `BRACE*let you gave me for* `CHRIST*mas goes* ˏwell *with it* `TOO, | `doesn't *it?*"

" `Yes," *I said.*

"*What on* `EARTH *are you doing to your* `HAIR?" *my mother asked.*

" 'Putting it 'on `top."

"*Oh, I* `DON'T *like* ⌄THAT," *my mother said.* "'Why are you 'doing it like `that?"

"*I* `like *it.*"

"*Your* `FATHer *won't* ˏlike *it," my mother said.* "'Good `heav*ens,* | *your stockings are trans*`PARent."

" `Yes."

" 'What's the 'good of 'wearing ↑ 'transparent 'stockings if your ↑ `legs *are blue?" my mother asked.* "'Are you 'going to 'wear your ˏboots | *and take your* `SHOES *with you in a* ⌄BAG?"

" `No," *I said.*

"*You've only got* 'five `MIN*utes* ˏnow," *my mother said.*

" `Yes, | *I* `know."

"*Will* ‚Sammy be there?" *my mother asked.*

"*I* ‚think so."

" 'Oh `good," *my mother said.* "*I* `hope you'll be nice and po`lite to ᵛHIM. *You* `will, | `won't you?"

" `Yes."

"*Yes,* `try," *my mother said.* "*Would you* 'like him to 'come to ‚tea?"

" ⁄No."

"*Oh,* `ALL ‚right," *my mother said.* "*But* `I think you're very `SILly, | `THAT'S ‚all. *I remember* `I didn't really like your `FATHer very ‚much | *when I* `FIRST ‚met him, | *but you* `WON'T take any notice of `ANything `I can ‚say. 'Can you ‚walk in those shoes?"

"`Yes."

"`Oh!" *my mother cried.* "*You're* 'not 'wearing your `vest! `HERE'S your ‚vest! 'Why have you 'taken it `off? `WHY aren't you wearing your vest?"

"*Because I'm* 'not `going to," *I said.*

"*Wear a* `CARDigan, ‚then," *my mother said.*

" *You'll be* `SOR‚ry," *my mother said,* | "*when the* `OTHers are all en`JOYing them‚selves | *and* `YOU'RE huddled over the ᵛFIRE | *with your* `TEETH ‚chattering | *and a* `RED ᵛNOSE | *and* `MAUVE ᵛHANDS. *Sammy* `WON'T find `THAT at‚tractive."

"*I'm* `READy ‚now," *I said.* "`Good-‚bye."

"*I'll* `PUT your hot-`WATer bottle **in**," *my mother said.*

"*En*`JOY your‚self, *Good*ᵛBYE."

Marjorie Riddell,
(From *Punch*, March 4th, 1953)

APPENDIX I

Verses for stress and rhythm practice.

The verses that follow are traditional children's rhymes and songs. They have well-defined patterns of stress and rhythm and are excellent material for practising these speech attributes. As they are verses, the stresses occur at unnaturally regular intervals, but this consistent regularity provides a good basis for practice in controlling the unstressed syllables that separate them. Each verse is to be read (or learnt by heart and recited) in strict rhythm, as if it were a piece of music. They can be spoken by single students or by larger groups in chorus.

Each verse will have its key rhythm set down in musical notation. To help the eye to catch this in reading, the syllable with the main stress will be marked with a high-pitch accent and will be printed in heavy type; the syllable with secondary stress will be marked with a low-pitch accent.

N.B.—The accents in this appendix have nothing to do with intonation.

Example: ˈ**Solo**mon ˌGrundy, ˈ**born** on ˌMonday,
ˈ**Christ**ened on ˌTuesday, ˈ**marri**ed on ˌWednesday. . . .

The teacher must insist that the stressed syllables follow one another in a strict, regular rhythm; if necessary, this can be tapped out on the desk. In a few of the later examples the pattern changes slightly for some lines; the music notation of such verses is given in full.

1. *Pattern:*

The |**north** wind doth |**blow** and |**we** shall have |**snow,**
And |**what** will poor |**rob**in do |**then,** poor |**thing**?
He'll |**sit** in a |**barn** and |**keep** himself |**warm,**
And |**hide** his head |**und**er his |**wing,** poor |**thing**!

2. *Pattern:*

  |**Jack** and Jill went |up the hill
  To |**fetch** a pail of |water,
  |**Jack** fell down and |broke his crown,
  And |**Jill** came tumbling |after.

3. *Pattern:*

|**Sol**omon |Grundy, |**born** on |Monday,
|**Christ**ened on |Tuesday, |**marr**ied on |Wednesday,
|**Fell** ill on |Thursday, |**worse** on |Friday,
|**Died** on |Saturday, |**bur**ied on |Sunday.
|**That** is the |end of |**Sol**omon |Grundy.

4. *Pattern:*

|**One,** |two, |**three,** four, |five, |**once** I |caught a |**fish**
  a|live.
|**Six,** |seven, |**eight,** nine, |ten, |**then** I |let him |**go**
  a|gain.
|**Why** |did you |**let** him |go? Be|**cause** he |bit my
  |**fing**er |so.
|**Which** |finger |**did** he |bite? The |**little** |finger |**on**
  the |right.

5. *Pattern:*

To ¹**mark**et, to ¹**mark**et, to ¹**buy** a fat ¹**pig**.
¹**Home** again, ¹**home** again, ¹**jiggety-**¹**jig**,
To ¹**mark**et, to ¹**mark**et, to ¹**buy** a fat ¹**hog**,
¹**Home** again, ¹**home** again, ¹**jiggety-**¹**jog**.

6. *Pattern:*

¹**Hot** ₁cross ¹**buns**, ¹**hot** ₁cross ¹**buns**,
¹**One** a ₁penny, ¹**two** a ₁penny, ¹**hot** ₁cross ¹**buns**.

(N.B. In the first line two secondary stresses are missing.
The reader must wait on the word "buns" for the whole of
this missing secondary stress, thus keeping syllables in
heavy type evenly spaced.)

7. *Pattern:*

¹**Lav**ender's ¹**blue**, dilly dilly, ¹**lav**ender's ¹**green**.
¹**When** I am ¹**king**, dilly dilly, ¹**you** shall be ¹**queen**.
¹**Call** up your ¹**men**, dilly dilly, ¹**set** them to ¹**work**,
¹**Some** with a ¹**rake**, dilly dilly, ¹**some** with a ¹**fork**.
¹**Some** to make ¹**hay**, dilly dilly, ¹**some** to thresh ¹**corn**,
¹**While** you and ¹**I**, dilly dilly, ¹**keep** ourselves ¹**warm**.

8. *Pattern:*

¹**Pease**-pudding ₁hot, ¹**pease**-pudding ₁cold,
¹**Pease**-pudding ₁in the pot ¹**nine** days ₁old.
¹**Some** like it ₁hot, ¹**some** like it ₁cold,
¹**Some** like it ₁in the pot ¹**nine** days ₁old.

9. *Pattern:*

Humpty ₁Dumpty **ˡsat** on a ₁wall,
ˡHumpty ₁Dumpty **ˡhad** a great ₁fall,
ˡAll the king's ₁horses and **ˡall** the king's ₁men
ˡCouldn't put ₁Humpty to₁**gether** a₁gain.

10. *Pattern:*

ˡOld King ₁Cole was a **ˡmerry** old ₁soul,
And a **ˡmerry** old ₁soul was **ˡhe.**
He **ˡcalled** for his ₁pipe and he **ˡcalled** for his ₁bowl,
And he **ˡcalled** for his ₁fiddlers **ˡthree.**

11. *Pattern:*

ˡJanuary ₁brings the snow, **ˡmakes** our feet and ₁fingers glow.
ˡFebruary ₁brings the rain, **ˡthaws** the frozen ₁lake again.
ˡMarch brings breezes ₁loud and shrill, **ˡstirs** the dancing ₁daffodil.
ˡApril brings the ₁primrose sweet, **ˡscatt**ers daisies ₁at our feet.
ˡMay brings flocks of ₁pretty lambs **ˡskip**ping by their ₁fleecy dams.
ˡJune brings tulips, ₁lilies, roses, **ˡfills** the children's ₁hands with posies.
ˡHot July brings ₁cooling showers, **ˡapr**icots and ₁gilly-flowers.
ˡAugust brings the ₁sheaves of corn, **ˡthen** the harvest ₁home is borne.

ǀ**Warm** September ǀbrings the fruit, ǀ**sports**men then
beǀgin to shoot.

ǀ**Fresh** October ǀbrings the pheasant, ǀ**then** to gather
ǀnuts is pleasant.

ǀ**Dull** November ǀbrings the blast, ǀ**then** the leaves are
ǀfalling fast.

ǀ**Chill** December ǀbrings the sleet, ǀ**blazing** fire and
ǀChristmas treat.

12. *Pattern:*

ǀ**Bat,** ǀbat, come ǀ**und**er my ǀhat
And I'll ǀ**give** you a ǀslice of ǀ**bacon**!
And ǀ**when** I ǀbake, I'll ǀ**give** you a ǀcake,
ǀ**If** I am ǀnot mis ǀ**taken.**

13. *Pattern:*

ǀ**Baa,** ǀbaa, ǀ**black** ǀsheep, ǀ**have** you ǀany ǀ**wool**?
ǀ**Yes,** ǀsir, ǀ**yes,** ǀsir, ǀ**three** ǀbags ǀ**full.**
ǀ**One** for my ǀ**mast**er, and ǀ**one** ǀfor my ǀ**dame,**
And ǀ**one** ǀfor the ǀ**little** ǀboy who ǀ**lives** ǀdown the
ǀ**lane.**

14. *Pattern:*

ǀ**George**ie ǀPorgie, ǀ**pud**ding and ǀpie,
ǀ**Kissed** the ǀgirls and ǀ**made** them ǀcry.
ǀ**When** the ǀboys came ǀ**out** to ǀplay,
ǀ**George**ie ǀPorgie ǀ**ran** aǀway.

15. *Pattern:*

To ˈbed, to ˌbed, says ˈSleepy-ˌhead,
ˈTarry a ˌwhile, says ˈSlow.
ˈPut on the ˌpan says ˈGreedy ˌNan,
Let's ˈsup beˌfore we ˈgo.

16. *Pattern:*

ˈHey diddle ˌdiddle, the ˈcat and the ˌfiddle
The ˈcow jumped ˌover the ˈmoon.
The ˈlittle dog ˌlaughed to ˈsee such ˌfun
And the ˈdish ran aˌway with the ˈspoon.

17. *Pattern:*

ˈOranges and ˈlemons, say the ˈbells of St. ˈClement's.
You ˈowe me five ˈfarthings, say the ˈbells of St.
  ˈMartin's.
ˈWhen will you ˈpay me? say the ˈbells of Old ˈBailey.
ˈWhen I grow ˈrich, say the ˈbells of Shoreˈditch.
ˈPray, when will ˈthat be? say the ˈsmall bells of
  ˈStepney.
I'm ˈsure I don't ˈknow, say the ˈgreat bells of ˈBow.

18. *Pattern:*

A ˈ**farm**er went ˌtrotting uˈ**pon** his grey ˌmare
ˈ**Bump**ety, ˌbumpety ˈ**bump**.
With his ˈ**daugh**ter beˌhind him so ˈ**ro**sy and ˌfair,
ˈ**Lump**ety, ˌlumpety ˌlump.

A ˈ**rav**en cried ˌCroak, and they ˈ**all** tumbled ˌdown,
ˈ**Bump**ety ˌbumpety ˈ**bump**.
The ˈ**mare** broke her ˌknees and the ˈ**farm**er his ˌcrown,
ˈ**Lump**ety ˌlumpety ˈ**lump**.

19. *Pattern:*

ˈ**Mon**day's child is ˌfair of face.
ˈ**Tues**day's child is ˌfull of grace
ˈ**Wedne**sday's child is ˌfull of woe.
ˈ**Thurs**day's child has ˌfar to go.
ˈ**Fri**day's child is ˌloving and giving.
ˈ**Sat**urday's child works ˌhard for its living.
But the ˈ**child** that is born on the ˌSabbath Day
Is ˈ**bon**ny and wise and ˌgood and gay.

20. *Pattern:*

ᶦ**Hark**, ₗhark, the ᶦ**dogs** do ₗbark,
The ᶦ**beg**gars are ₗcoming to ᶦ**town**;
ᶦ**Some** in ₗrags and ᶦ**some** in ₗtags
And ᶦ**one** in a ₗvelvet ᶦ**gown**.

APPENDIX II
Syllable Stress

The accentuation of long words is very irregular in English and is a constant source of trouble to the student. It is not possible to give any certain rules for the position of the stress in longer words, but the following hints and generalizations may be of help.

N.B.—Accents in this appendix refer to stress only, not intonation.

1. **Germanic compounds.**

   The stress almost always remains on the original root.

   Examples with suffixes:
   ˈdrunkard, ˈspeaker, ˈlaughing-stock, ˈfishmonger, ˈplaywright, ˈheathendom, ˈneighbourhood, ˈcallousness, ˈwonderful, ˈoutward.

   Examples with prefixes:
   beˈside, beˈwilder, foreˈsee, misunderˈstand, overˈheated, unˈpleasant.

   Important exceptions are:
   toˈward, ˈforeground, ˈforecast, ˈforehead, ˈupkeep, ˈupbringing, and a few other nouns and adjectives with *fore* or *up*.

2. **Classical compounds**

   The stress of these is less easy to guess, but a few suffixes make words of a pattern regular enough to be worth mentioning.

-**ion**, taking a stress on the preceding syllable.

ocˈcasion, paˈvilion, perˈsuasion, proˈmotion, calcuˈlation, etc.

Exceptions:

The scientific terms: ˈcation, ˈanion, (kætaiǝn, ˈænaiǝn), and ˈdandelion. -*ion* is not a suffix in these words.

-**ic(al)**, as above.

ˈcomic(al), faˈnatic(al), ˈtragic, ecoˈnomic(al), etc.

Six important exceptions are the words: ˈcatholic, ˈheretic, ˈlunatic, ˈarabic, aˈrithmetic, ˈrhetoric.

Note also the following noun-adjective pairs:

ˈheretic, heˈretical; ˈrhetoric, rheˈtorical; ˈpolitics, poˈlitical; aˈrithmetic, arithˈmetic(al).

The following two-syllable suffixes almost always take a stress on the syllable immediately preceding:

-ian, -ial, -cient, -ious, -eous, -ual, -uous, -ity, -ety, -itous, -itive, -itude, -itant.

-ate, *verbs only, three syllables or more, have antepenultimate stress, i.e. third syllable from the end:*

ˈagitate, ˈdeviate, apˈpreciate, eˈvaporate, inˈterpolate, ilˈluminate, etc.

Note: inˈterrogate and interˈrogative.

-fy, *verbs only, three syllables or more, as above:*

perˈsonify, ˈqualify, ˈstupefy, ˈglorify, ˈterrify, etc.

-ize (*or* -ise), *verbs only, three syllables or more, as above:*

aˈpologize, moˈnopolize, ˈjeopardize, ˈsubsidize, etc.

Exceptions are mostly modern coinings, e.g. ˈregularize, ˈcharacterize, *and the very recent* ˈhospitalize.

Note that verbs of **two** syllables under the last **three** headings have end-stress:

inˈflate, surˈprise, bapˈtize, deˈfy.

3. Antepenultimate stress

The long and rather uncommon word used in this paragraph heading literally "speaks for itself". Listen to it. ˈAntepen-ˈultimate (strong-weak-weak, strong-weak-weak). The stress is on the third syllable from the end, which results in a classical dactylic rhythm (–ᴜᴜ).

This stress and the rhythm that follows from it seem to suit the English language. If we remember that the suffix -ic is also -ical, and that -tion, -lion, -sion, etc., were pronounced as two syllables until at least the end of the seventeenth century, we shall find that antepenultimate stress is common to a very large proportion of words of more than three syllables, excluding Germanic compounds (see Exercise 150). Notice the large number of words in section 2 that have this stress.

The tendency in the living language to change the stress so that it ultimately falls into this position is a further indication that the English find it comfortable and natural to say the words in this way. Here are a few examples of this tendency at work.

(i) Words whose stress has moved one syllable back within the last 80 years or so:

ˈblasphemous, ˈcontrary, ˈcharacter, ˈquandary, ˈbalcony, ˈpergola, ˈgondola, ˈcontemplate (cf. conˈtemplative), ˈmassacre, ˈparasol (*two syllables from* paraˈsol).

(ii) Some words that have more recently adopted this stress:

Older form	*Newly established form*
anˈchovy [ænˈtʃouvi]	ˈanchovy [ˈæntʃəvi]
alˈly (n.) [əˈlai]	ˈally (n.) [ˈælai]
abˈdomen [æbˈdoumen]	ˈabdomen [ˈæbdəmen]
comˈbine (n.) [kəmˈbain]	ˈcombine[1] [ˈkɔmbain]

[1] *As* ˈbusiness ˈcombine *or* ˈcombine ˈharvester.

obli'gatory [ɔbli'geitəri]   o'bligatory [ə'bligətri]
re'condite [ri'kɔndait]   'recondite ['rekəndait]
'metallurgy ['metələ:dʒi]   me'tallurgy [me'tælədʒi]
'nomenclature   no'menclature
   ['noumənkleitʃə]   [no'menklətʃə]
va'gary [və'gɛəri]   'vagary ['veigəri]
'controversy ['kɔntrəvə:si]   con'troversy [kən'trɔvəsi]
re'plica [re'pli:kə]   'replica ['replikə]
frag'mentary [fræg'mentəri]   'fragmentary ['frægməntri]
   [frəg'mentəri]
pre'cedence [pri'si:dəns]   'precedence ['presidəns]

Both forms of some of the above are still to be heard.

(iii) Some words that are apparently in the process of changing stress:

Standard form	*Modern variant*
tra'jectory [trə'dʒektəri]	'trajectory ['trædʒiktri]
'applicable ['æplikəbl]	ap'plicable [ə'plikəbl]
'hospitable ['hɔspitəbl]	hos'pitable [hɔs'pitəbl]
'kilometre ['kiləˌmi:tə]	ki'lometre [ki'lɔmitə]
tra'chea [trə'kiə]	'trachea ['treikiə]
'exigency ['eksidʒənsi]	ex'igency [ig'zidʒənsi]
eti'quette [eti'ket]	'etiquette ['etiket]
pro'jectile (n.) [prə'dʒektail]	'projectile ['prɔdʒəktail]
ob'durate [ɔb'dju:rət]	'obdurate ['ɔbdjurət]

One might notice also the common change of stress when two-syllable words grow into longer ones: *e.g.*

'pious—'impious—im'piety ['paiəs, 'impiəs, im'paiəti].
'thesis—an'tithesis ['θi:sis, æn'tiθisis].
'potent—'impotent—om'nipotent ['poutənt, 'impətənt, ɔm'nipətənt].

Here are some word-sequences to practise this shifting of the stress to the antepenultimate syllable.

Exercise 146 (advanced vocabulary)

Read aloud each word of the following sequences two or three times. Place a strong accent on the syllable in bold type *and be careful to read other syllables in their unstressed (weak) forms. (Look at the phonetic transcription if you are in doubt.)*

politics / po**li**tical / poli**ti**cian
democrat / de**moc**racy / demo**crat**ic
personal / per**son**ify / perso**nal**ity
hypocrite / hy**poc**risy / hypo**crit**ical
photograph / pho**tog**rapher / photo**graph**ical
benefit / be**nef**icent / bene**fic**ial
mechanism / me**chan**ical / mecha**nic**ian / mechani**za**tion
contemplate / con**temp**lative / contem**pla**tion
meteor / mete**or**ic / meteo**rol**ogy / metero**log**ical
artifice / ar**tif**icer / arti**fic**ial / artificiality
antiquate / an**tiq**uity / anti**quar**ian
intellect / in**tell**igence / intel**lec**tual / intelli**gent**sia
family / fa**mil**iar / famili**ar**ity
telegraph / te**leg**raphy / tele**graph**ic
philanthrop / phi**lan**thropist / philan**throp**ical
particle / par**tic**ular / particu**lar**ity
competence / com**pet**itor / compe**ti**tion
diplomat / dip**lom**acy / diplo**mat**ic

Phonetic guide to Exercise 146

ˈpɒlitiks pəˈlitikl pɒliˈtiʃn / ˈdemɒkræt diˈmɔkrəsi ˌdemoˈkrætik / ˈpəːsənəl pəˈsɔnifai pəːsəˈnæliti / ˈhipɒkrit hiˈpɒkrisi hipoˈkritikl / ˈfoutəgrɑːf fəˈtɔgrəfə foutəˈgræfikl / ˈbenifit biˈnefisənt beniˈfiʃl / ˈmekənizm miˈkænikl mekəˈniʃn ˌmekənaiˈzeiʃn / ˈkɔntəmpleit kənˈtemplətiv kɔntəmˈpleiʃn / ˈmiːtiə miːtiˈɔrik miːtjəˈrɔlədʒi ˌmiːtjərəˈlɔdʒikl / ˈɑːtifis ɑːˈtifisə ˌɑːtiˈfiʃl ˌɑːtifiʃiˈæliti / ˈæntikweit ænˈtikwiti æntiˈkwɛəriən / ˈintilekt inˈtelidʒəns intiˈlektjuəl

ˌinteliˈdʒentsiə / ˈfæm(i)li fəˈmiljə fəmiliˈæriti / ˈteligrɑːf tiˈlegrəfi ˌteliˈgræfik / ˈfilənərɔp fiˈlænərəpist filənˈərəpikl / ˈpɑːtikl pəˈtikjulə pətikjuˈlæriti / ˈkɔmpitəns kəmˈpetitə kɔmpiˈtiʃn / ˈdipləmæt diˈplouməsi (*or* diˈplɔməsi) diplə-ˈmætik.

One final indication of the naturalness of this stress in English can be seen in the very large number of long words where this stress is placed on a syllable that completely disguises the real meaning of the word. For instance, the printed word "photographer" (see Exercise 146) is perfectly obvious to most foreigners who know a European language. Its pronunciation, however (fəˈtɔgrəfə) leads their ears to imagine a mysterious root called "tog", giving no clue to the component parts of the word. Here is a number of such "disguised" words for practice:

Exercise 147 (advanced vocabulary)

Read each of the following words three times, emphasizing the stressed syllable in **bold type.**

moˈ**not**onous, libeˈ**ral**ity, teˈ**leph**onist, auˈ**ton**omy, eˈ**quiv**ocal, teˈ**leg**raphy, geneˈ**ros**ity, seniˈ**or**ity, magˈ**nan**imous, magna**nim**ity, baˈ**rom**eter, therˈ**mom**eter, peˈ**rim**eter, heˈ**xam**eter, chroˈ**nom**eter, ˈ**sec**retary, saˈ**gac**ity, eˈ**pit**ome, caˈ**tas**trophe, maˈ**nip**ulate, noˈ**bil**ity, noˈ**nen**tity, omˈ**ni**scient, parˈ**tic**ular, coˈ**med**ian, Caˈ**na**dian, theˈ**los**ophy, geˈ**ol**ogy, geˈ**og**raphy, boˈ**tan**ical, gramˈ**mat**ical, laˈ**bor**atory, elasˈ**tic**ity, sigˈ**nif**icant, lonˈ**gev**ity.

Phonetic guide to Exercise 147

məˈnɔtənəs, libəˈræliti, tiˈlefənist, ɔːˈtɔnəmi, iˈkwivəkl, tiˈlegrəfi, dʒenəˈrɔsiti, siːniˈɔriti, məgˈnæniməs, mægnə-ˈnimiti, bəˈrɔmitə, θəˈmɔmitə, pəˈrimitə, hekˈsæmitə, krəˈnɔmitə, ˈsekrətri, səˈgæsiti, iˈpitəmi, kəˈtæstrəfi, məˈnipjuleit, noˈbiliti, nɔˈnentiti, omˈnisiənt, pəˈtikjulə, kəˈmiːdiən, kəˈneidiən, θiˈɔsəfi, dʒiˈɔlədʒi, dʒiˈɔgrəfi, bəˈtænikl, grəˈmætikl, ləˈbɔrətri, ˌiːlæsˈtisiti, sigˈnifikənt, lɔnˈdʒeviti.

This last section, which concerns itself with the tendency for English speakers to feel a certain natural ease in ante-penultimate stress for the pronunciation of longer words of classical origin, is not to be taken as a reliable guide to the correct accentuation of all such words. There are too many exceptions. A student who is not sure of the right way to stress some long word should ask an English speaker or consult a reliable dictionary. The shifting of stress as new suffixes add extra syllables, and the fact that this stress so commonly settles on the third syllable from the end ir-respective of the meaningful stressing of the word's component parts, make Exercises 146 and 147 useful reading tasks for intermediate and more advanced students; for it is only when the stress falls on an unexpected syllable that a foreign speaker finds a long word difficult to say correctly. The teacher should also insist on the correct weak forms of the unstressed syllables, and it is for that purpose that a phonetic key has been added to these two exercises.

4. Secondary stress in longer words (*mostly non-Germanic*)

Words of more than three syllables usually take a secondary stress as well as the principal one. This normally falls on the first or second syllable, and is much weaker than the main stress; but the vowel-sound is always given its full value. There are no certain rules for finding this stress, but as it is important for the natural shape and rhythm of longer words, the following two lists of typical examples are given for reading practice.

Exercise 148 (advanced vocabulary)

Read each of the following words twice or three times, with a strong stress on the syllable in **bold type** *and a weaker stress on the first syllable:*

ˌrelaˈtivity, ˌvegeˈtarian, ˌcharacteˈristic, ˌpsychoˈlogical, ˌtotaliˈtarian, ˌcrystalliˈzation, ˌsuperannuˈation, ˌqualifiˈcation, ˌheteroˈgeneous, ˌantepenˈultimate, ˌcancelˈlation, ˌautobiˈography, ˌcontraˈdiction, ˌhesiˈtation, ˌindeˈpendent, ˌmonuˈmental, ˌnaturaliˈzation, ˌdisoˈbedient, ˌsuperimˈpose, ˌoverˈwhelming, ˌdiaˈbolical, ˌparalˈlelogram, ˌunderˈstanding, ˌpropaˈganda, ˌrehabiliˈtation, ˌinterˈnational, ˌmicroˈscopic, ˌadvanˈtageous, ˌtheoˈretical, ˌversaˈtility, ˌinconˈgruity, ˌrecommenˈdation, ˌirreˈdentist, ˌincompreˈhensible, ˌcontiˈnuity, ˌemiˈgration, ˌsuperˈstitious, ˌaristoˈcratic, ˌproleˈtarian.

Exercise 149 (advanced vocabulary)

Read each of the following words twice or three times, with a strong stress on the syllable in **bold type** *and a weaker stress on the second syllable:*

proˌnunciˈation, adˌminisˈtration, exˌamiˈnation, oˌrigiˈnality, acˌcomoˈdation, maˌteriaˈlistic, conˌtinuˈation, Naˌpoleˈonic, peˌculiˈarity, perˌsonifiˈcation, poˌtentiˈality, eˌvacuˈation, disˌcrimiˈnation, exˌpostuˈlation, reˌsponsiˈbility, asˌsimiˈlation, inˌcorrigiˈbility, imˌperiaˈlistic, eˌxaggeˈration, conˌtempoˈraneous, oˌbliteˈration, irˌrevocaˈbility, proˌcrastiˈnation, inˌflexiˈbility, eˌlectrifiˈcation.

Note on extremely long English words of non-Germanic origin.

Words of more than 5 syllables are not very commonly used in speech. They generally have another principal stress on the first or second syllable, as well as a weaker (secondary) stress towards the middle. Examples of this pattern are: ˈexcomˌmuniˈcation, ˈsuperˌeroˈgation, ˈantiˌviviˈsection.

5. Stressing of juxtapositional compound nouns

The joining together of separate words to make a compound is an important English speech device. The new compound may remain as two (or more) words, or be joined by a hyphen, or be written as a single word. We are not concerned here with the grammatical relations of the component parts, nor with orthography. We shall merely note that the resulting compound noun is usually spoken with a single stress on the first part only, the other syllables sounding low and unstressed.

Exercise 150 (fairly advanced vocabulary)

Read each of the following compounds twice or three times, stressing only the syllable in **bold type.** *Take care that all the other syllables are without stress and on a low tone.*

Example: ˈsteamship company.

ˈFishing boat, ˈtennis racquet, ˈbathing costume, ˈdinnerplate, ˈdoorhandle, ˈplayingfield, ˈnursery school, ˈopera house, ˈcandlepower, ˈblotting paper, ˈbicycle-pump, ˈfactory worker, poˈlice station, ˈrailway station, ˈtelegraph pole, ˈsticking plaster, ˈairmail envelope, ˈtypewriter, ˈcushion cover, ˈpaper-fastener, ˈtraffic control, ˈtoothbrush-holder, ˈsports ground, ˈsymphony orchestra, ˈpencil sharpener, ˈsewing-machine, ˈhandbag, ˈlightning conductor, ˈlodginghouse-keeper, ˈradio technician, ˈshoe repairer, ˈbroadcasting station, ˈsmoking-compartment, ˈsecondary-school teacher, ˈrecord-breaker, ˈeyewitness,

ǀ**note**worthy,   ǀ**walk**ing-stick,   ǀ**step**ping-stone,   ǀ**after**-thought,   ǀ**on**looker,   ǀ**whole**sale department,   ǀ**furn**iture-polish,   ǀ**furn**iture-polish manufacturer.

6. Stress and grammar

It is a well-known grammatical fact that some words have different functions according to whether they are given a full or weak pronunciation. Common words of this type are " one ", " that ", and " some ". There is also a large class of words, mostly of two syllables, which take end-stress as verbs and forward-stress as nouns or adjectives. Here are two lists of the more usual words of this class, put into short sentences to help show the meaning :

Exercise 151.

List 1 (more usual words)

1. CONFLICT
   It was a **con**flict between his wishes and his duties.
   These dates con**flict** with my arrangements.

2. CONTRACT
   He has signed a new **con**tract with the firm.
   Metals con**tract** as the temperature falls.

3. EXTRACT
   He read us an **ex**tract from his new book.
   They will never ex**tract** a confession from him.

4. TRANSPORT
   The **trans**port of heavy goods is expensive.
   We can't trans**port** the whole of the furniture.

5. EXPORT
   This article is for **ex**port only.
   We try to ex**port** as much as possible.

6. IMPORT
   You will require an **im**port licence.
   We have to im**port** a great deal of food.

7. CONTRAST

She likes strong **con**trasts of colour.
The critic con**trast**ed their styles of writing.

8. ABSENT

He was **ab**sent from class last week.
You shouldn't ab**sent** yourself from class.

9. TRANSFER

He's expecting a **trans**fer to another office.
You can trans**fer** the property to your brother.

10. PROGRESS

You have made good (slow) **pro**gress in English.
The work will pro**gress** gradually.

11. CONVERSE

If that is so, the **con**verse is also true.
They tried to con**verse** in English.

12. INCREASE

We expect an **in**crease of work next week.
Their numbers continue to in**crease**.

13. DECREASE

There's a **de**crease in the number of students in our
class.
Our numbers continue to de**crease**.

14. PRESENT

We are all **pre**sent today to give him a **pre**sent.
We shall pre**sent** him with a watch.

15. RECORD

A gramophone **rec**ord. A sports **rec**ord.
These instruments re**cord** weather conditions.

16. CONDUCT

His friends defended his **con**duct.
He will con**duct** you to the president.

17. PRODUCE
    Farm **prod**uce can be bought at the market.
    They pro**duce** all kinds of glassware.

18. CONTEST
    Many people watched the final **con**test.
    We shall con**test** his right to the property.

19. SUSPECT
    They are holding him as a **sus**pect.
    They sus**pect** him of theft.

20. SUBJECT
    He's taking English as his main **sub**ject.
    They'll sub**ject** the book to careful criticism.

21. PERFECT
    He speaks with a **per**fect accent.
    He's in England to per**fect** his accent.

22. CONVICT
    The **con**vict escaped from prison.
    They are sure to con**vict** him of the crime.

23. PROTEST
    They made a **pro**test against the decision.
    He will pro**test** against it.

24. CONVERT
    He was a **con**vert to our faith.
    Heat will con**vert** water into steam.

25. DESERT
    He crossed the **des**ert in a jeep.[1]
    Don't de**sert** us now that we need you.

26. ENVELOP(E)
    Put the letter in the **en**velope. (1st syllable.)
    They were en**vel**oped in a cloud of dust. (2nd syllable.)

---

[1] But notice the noun from "deserve": He got his de**serts**.

27. OBJECT
 An ear-ring is not a useful **ob**ject.
 I ob**ject** to your last remark.

28. PERFUME
 I like the **per**fume you are using tonight.
 The carnations per**fume** the evening air.

29. REBEL
 A **reb**el fights against existing authority.
 We must re**bel** against these stupid conventions.

30. INSULT
 This act is an **in**sult to our people.
 He didn't mean to in**sult** us.

31. ALLY
 He was a faithful **al**ly.
 We shall al**ly** ourselves to them.

32. COMBINE
 It is part of a large business **com**bine.
 Hydrogen and oxygen com**bine** to form water.

33. DICTATE
 She followed the **dic**tates of her heart.
 I'll dic**tate** the letter to you.

34. DISCOURSE
 We enjoy friendly **dis**course.
 We dis**coursed** on many topics.

35. ESCORT
 A naval **es**cort was in attendance.
 May I es**cort** you to your room?

36. EXPLOIT
 We enjoy hearing about your **ex**ploits.
 We must not ex**ploit** his good will.

37. FREQUENT

> There were **fre**quent showers all day.
> I used to fre**quent** such cafés.

38. PERMIT

> You'll need a **per**mit to fish here.
> Will you per**mit** me to say a few words?

39. SURVEY

> Let us make a **sur**vey of the situation.
> Let us sur**vey** the situation.

40. INCLINE

> The ball rolled down the **in**cline.
> I am in**clined** to believe him.

Exercise 152.

List 2 (less usual words)

1. REJECT

> He bought it as an **ex**port **re**ject.
> They may re**ject** your claim for damages.

2. ABSTRACT

> Here is an **abs**tract of the whole argument.
> His arrival ab**stract**ed our attention from the speech.

3. DIGEST

> Give me a **di**gest of their speeches.
> I can't di**gest** too much fat.

4. IMPRESS

> The letter bore the **im**press of the chancellor's office.
> His manner did not im**press** me.

5. COMPRESS

> He soothed the sprain with a cold **com**press.
> We must com**press** it into a smaller space.

6. OVERFLOW

There was an **over**flow of people into the courtyard.
The river may over**flow**.

7. REDRESS

There'll be no **re**dress for this wrong.
They hope to re**dress** the wrong they have done.

8. ATTRIBUTE

Mercy is an **at**tribute of a generous mind.
They at**trib**ute this poem to Chaucer.

9. PROSPECT

There is but little **pros**pect of his returning.
He left to pros**pect** for gold.

10. ACCENT

His English **ac**cent is very good.
[1]You should ac**cent** the final syllable.

11. ADDICT

He is, I fear, a drug **ad**dict.
He is ad**dict**ed to taking drugs.

12. CONSCRIPT

He is a new **con**script.
[2]He has been con**script**ed (into the army).

13. ADVERT

I answered an **ad**vert. in the personal column.

(colloq.)

The judge ad**vert**ed to the counsel's remarks. (liter.)

14. UPSET

Their sudden arrival caused quite an **up**set.
The waves up**set** the little boat.

---

[1] But there is a growing tendency to stress the first syllable for both noun and verb.

[2] The verb *con'scribe* (to enlist compulsorily) seems to have given way to a new verb *to con'script* (from the noun *'conscript* or *con'scription.*)

15. CONCERT
    I am fond of orchestral **con**certs.
    Our con**cert**ed efforts brought success.

16. CONFINE(S)
    The talk extended to the **con**fines of philosophy.
    He was con**fined** to his room with a cold.

17. CONSORT
    The king and his **con**sort were warmly welcomed.
    You shouldn't con**sort** with such people.

18. DETAIL
    They could see every **de**tail in the picture.
    He couldn't de**tail** all the facts.

19. AFFIX
    "Over" is an **af**fix in "overlook".
    You must af**fix** your signature to this document.

20. CONSOLE
    He was sitting at the organ **con**sole.
    She tried to con**sole** the lost child.

21. REFUSE
    All **ref**use should be burnt. [ˈrefjuːs]
    He may re**fuse** to tell you. [riˈfjuːz]

22. TORMENT
    These flies are a great **tor**ment.
    The flies tor**ment** us a lot here.

23. INCENSE
    The church smelt of **in**cense.
    We were in**censed** by his rudeness.

24. ESSAY
    He's writing an **ess**ay on H. G. Wells.
    We must es**say** this task (liter.)

25. ENTRANCE

The **en**trance is through the other door. [ˈentrəns]

Her performance will en**trance** you. [enˈtrɑ:ns]

26. RETAIL

We got it at the **re**tail price.

He **retailed** the whole adventure.

27. DEFILE

They walked miles along a narrow **def**ile.

Such remarks de**file** her character.

28. DESCANT

She sang a **des**cant above the melody.

He des**cant**ed for hours upon these problems.

29. DISCOUNT

He gave me five per cent **dis**count.

We must dis**count** his highly coloured report.

30. CONTENT(S)

Here's a list of the **con**tents.

You must con**tent** yourself with that.

Note. Although the verb/noun change of stress provides the most examples, there are some other pairs of words that are differentiated by stress in a similar manner. Here are a few of the more important ones:

ˈ**Au**gust (n), au**gust** (adj.), al**tern**ate (adj.) **alter**nate (vb.) **com**pact (n), com**pact** (adj.), **min**ute (n), mi**nute** [maiˈnju:t] (adj.), **in**valid (n), in**val**id (adj.), to **con**jure (juggle), to con**jure** (entreat).

There are also several pairs of phrases, one of which has formed a single-stress compound, the other retaining the normal two stresses of adjective and noun. A few examples are:

ˈground ˈnuts (nuts chopped fine)

ˈgroundnuts (peanuts)

a ˈgreenˈfly (fly of a green colour)
                    a ˈgreenfly (aphis)
a ˈˈleather ˈjacket (made of leather)
                    a ˈˈleatherjacket (larva of cranefly)
a ˈblack ˈbird (a bird of a black colour)
                    a ˈblackbird (a singing bird, *Turdus merula*)
a ˈcopper ˈplate (made of copper)
                    a ˈcopperplate (engraving)

7. Level-stress words

A large number of words, mostly compounds, take two even stresses (the second one falling) when they stand isolated, as in a dictionary. When such words are used in connected speech, they regularly lose one of their stresses according to the following pattern.

(i) When final, and immediately preceded by a stress, the word loses its own first stress.

(ii) When a stress immediately follows the word, it loses its own second stress.

(iii) When a stress both precedes and follows the word, it often loses both its own stresses. If it is felt necessary to give it some prominence, the first stress is the one normally retained.

Examples: ˈsixˋteen (isolated or dictionary form)

  (i) She's ˈjust sixˋteen.

  (ii) It's ˈsixteen ˋmiles.

  (iii) We've ˈover sixteen ˈmiles to ˋgo,
    or We've ˈover ˈsixteen ˈmiles to ˋgo.

Exercise 153.

Read aloud the following pairs of sentences containing level-stress words in varying positions. The relevant stresses will be shown in **bold type**:

1. The ˈBudapest ˈcliˈmate's of a ˈcontinental ˈtype.
   He ˈlives in Budaˈpest. The ˈclimate's contiˈnental.
2. ˈHave a ˈpiece of ˈhome-made ˈcake. This ˈcake's
   home-ˈmade.
3. He has ˈfive o'clock ˈtea nearly ˈevery afterˈnoon.
   He has ˈafternoon ˈtea. It's ˈnearly five o'ˈclock.
4. There's a ˈman downˈstairs; he's ˈcome from New
   ˈYork.
   A ˈNew York ˈjournalist ˈlives in the ˈdownstairs
   ˈroom.
5. We ˈwatched the ˈchanging of the ˈBuckingham
   Palace ˈguards.
   It's ˈnear Buckingham ˈPalace. It's ˈnot very far
   from ˈBuckingham ˈPalace.[1]
6. He's ˈjust a ˈsilly, ˈempty-headed ˈboy.
   He ˈnever reˈmembers ˈanything; he's ˈquite empty-
   ˈheaded.
7. He ˈgave me an ˈoff-hand ˈanswer.
   Well, ˈthat's his ˈnature; he's ˈalways off-ˈhand.
8. ˈWhy didn't you ˈhurry? ˈNow your ˈsoup's stone-
   ˈcold.
   Well, ˈstone-cold ˈsoup's very ˈnice in this ˈhot
   ˈweather.
9. The ˈsight of a ˈdistant ˈship ˈraised our ˈhopes of
   salˈvation.
   She does ˈfine ˈwork in the ˈSalvation ˈArmy.
10. I'll ˈgive you a ˈpost-dated ˈcheque. ˈBy the ˈway, I
    ˈhope you don't ˈmind it's ˈbeing post-ˈdated.
11. " ˈHow can such a ˈgood-natured ˈwoman ˈhave such
    a ˈbad-tempered ˈdaughter? The ˈmother's ex-
    ˈtremely good-ˈnatured, but the ˈgirl's unbeˈliev-
    ably bad-ˈtempered."

[1] B.P. is here isolated, and so has its two stresses. If the previous stress
is made to fall on "far" instead of "not", the stress on "Buckingham"
will be very much weakened.

12. "She's |also cross-|eyed, not to |mention knock-
    |knee'd, which |doesn't |add to her at|tractions.
    But, of |course, there's |no reason |why a |cross-
    eyed or |knock-knee'd |person should |also be bad-
    |tempered."

13. "|What's that |reddish-brown |object over |there
    among the |trees?"
    "I |think it's a |deer; but it |looks to |me more |grey
    than reddish-|brown."

14. "Is |this |hot enough for |you to |shave with? I'm
    a|fraid it's |only luke|warm."
    "I |don't like |shaving with |lukewarm |water, but
    it's |better than |nothing."

15. They |crossed Hyde |Park and |waited at |Hyde
    Park |Corner.

16. He has a |charming little |week-end |cottage. He
    |goes there |every week-|end.

17. She's |wearing her |navy blue |costume. I |always
    |think she |looks her |best in navy |blue.

18. The |sardine |sandwiches were de|licious, but the
    to|matoes were |all over|ripe. |Overripe |fruit gets
    |squashed easily. I |love sar|dines!

19. "|Do you like |underdone |meat?"
    "|Not |usually. Ex|cept |steak, which I |like |very
    under|done."

20. I |want a |third-class |ticket to King's |Cross. I
    |always |go third-|class.
    |King's Cross |Station is a |London |terminus.

21. There's a |good-looking |girl over |there in a |light
    blue |hat.
    She's |quite good-|looking; her |hat's light |blue.

22. He |leads an |anti-social |life; he does |illegal |business
    on the |local black |market. His |black market |deals
    are |quite il|legal; |that's why I |say it's anti-|social.

23. It's a concert by the 'Belgrade 'Symphony Orchestra.
    It's 'near Bel'grade.

24. She has 'artificial 'eyelashes; her 'pearls are arti-
    'ficial.

25. The 'upstairs 'room has an 'outside 'staircase.
    He 'lives up'stairs; there's a 'bell out'side.

26. Our 'absent-minded pro'fessor wears a 'second-hand
    'wig.
    Our pro'fessor's absent-'minded and his 'wig is
    second-'hand.

27. He's 'inside 'right for the 'Berlin 'team.
    'Put it 'right in'side; it's 'made in Ber'lin.

28. He's an 'unknown 'member of a 'diplomatic 'mis-
    sion.
    Be 'very diplo'matic as he's 'quite un'known.

29. "It's a 'shop in Picca'dilly—a 'well-known 'Picca-
    dilly 'jeweller's."
    "Yes, it's 'quite well-'known. 'How do I 'get there?"
    "Well, it's 'not so 'far from 'Piccadilly 'Circus. You
    can 'get out at 'Piccadilly Circus 'Station."

30. He was 'born in 1919. ('nineteen—nine'teen.)

Note. A similar rhythmical variation of stress is found with
phrasal verbs (simple verbs with adverb particles). Notice
the variation in the following:

to 'take 'off; to 'put 'on.
He 'took his 'coat off; he 'took it 'off; 'John took it 'off: he
'put it 'on; 'John put his 'coat on; 'John put it 'on.

INDEX

Numbers refer to exercises and their notes.